Apostasy and Jewish identity
in High Middle Ages Northern Europe

Manchester University Press

Apostasy and Jewish identity in High Middle Ages Northern Europe

'Are you still my brother?'

Simha Goldin
Translated by Jonathan Chipman

Manchester University Press

Published by Manchester University Press
Altrincham Street, Manchester M1 7JA, UK
www.manchesteruniversitypress.co.uk

British Library Cataloguing-in-Publication Data
A catalogue record for this book is available from the British Library

Library of Congress Cataloging-in-Publication Data applied for

ISBN   978 0 7190 9577 1   hardback

First published 2014

The publisher has no responsibility for the persistence or accuracy of URLs for any external or third-party internet websites referred to in this book, and does not guarantee that any content on such websites is, or will remain, accurate or appropriate.

Typeset
by Carnegie Book Production, Lancaster
Printed in Great Britain
by TJ International Ltd, Padstow

Contents

Preface

O ver the course of the last two generations, thousands of people all over the world saw the musical *Fiddler on the Roof*, and at the end found themselves giving it a standing ovation, their eyes wet with tears.[1] Everyone who saw it identified with the moving story of a middle-aged man who was forced to deal with the changes occurring in the world around him, as reflected in the lives of his daughters.

The musical *Fiddler on the Roof* is based upon the book *Tevye der Milkhiker* ('Tevye the Milkman'), written by the Yiddish author Shalom Rabinowitz, better known by his pen name Shalom Aleikhem ('peace upon you'), the greeting with which two Jews meeting one another identify as Jews. Rabinowitz was born in 1859 in the town of Pereyaslav in the Kiev district. In 1905, he immigrated to the New World; he died in New York City in 1916. From 1894 on he began to publish the adventures of Tevye the Milkman in serialized form and, for the rest of his life, never ceased to be engaged with this work, expanding it, and dealing with various questions related to its structure, characters, and plot.

Shalom Aleikhem's Tevye was forced to deal with a new and changing world, and with his seven daughters, each one of whom challenged him with a truth of her own. The first preferred romantic love with a life of poverty to an arranged match without love to an established and wealthy husband; the second fell in love with a fearless Jewish revolutionary who tried to change society and ended up in a harsh and remote prison in Siberia where she, out of her intense love, joined him. The third committed suicide due to her love for a man who submitted to the pressures of society and cut off their romantic connection; while a fourth married a wealthy husband in order to help provide for her poor family.

But the heart of the story is doubtless Tevye's confrontation with his beloved daughter Chava, who fell in love with a Polish Christian, and married him in church, as a Christian, thereby abandoning her family, her religion, and her father who loved her like his own soul. The father, in a complex, touching, and tragic chapter, describes the affair, recounting his own attempts to return her to him and to her Jewishness in light of the priest's joy at his 'victory.' When the dimensions of his theological failure as a father become clear to him, he carries out the ultimate act of the Jew, cutting himself off from Chava in a final and decisive manner. He declares his converted daughter to be dead, rends his garments, and sits *shivah* for her. 'There is no Chava, Chava is dead,' and goes on with his life.

At the end of the story it becomes clear to the Jewish family, who have lived their entire lives in a Christian village, that times have changed and that they are now to be expelled from the village. Tevye takes his family, his daughters, and grandchildren, and leaves the village forever. Thus are Jews expelled. Then, at the height of the drama of the expulsion, his Christian daughter Chava suddenly appears in their home to inform him that she is leaving everything and coming back to him, to be expelled along with him. A deep understanding of the reality of Jewish life in the world envelops both father and daughter. Chava realizes that the Jew always remains a Jew and cannot alter his religion for another, and that the Gentiles will never accept either the Jew who remains a Jew or the Jew who has converted to Christianity. Chava symbolizes the entire process through her very being. She took the Christian religion upon herself out of love for a Christian boy and became aware that her act is opposed to the way of the world. Now that the Jews are being expelled, as always by the Christians, she abandons her new religion and returns to the old one. Tevye learns what Rashi had stated centuries earlier: that a Jew, even if he becomes an apostate, remains a Jew. Despite what Chava said in church, despite her taking upon herself the principles of her new religion, her essence has not changed: she remains a Jew. Thus, the rending of the garments, the sitting *shivah*, and the recitation of Kaddish, did not nullify Chava's life as a Jew, and she remained a Jew, stayed alive, and returned.

The scene in which Tevye confronts his daughter's conversion to Christianity came from the very heart of the author, who returns to this episode repeatedly. Even while living in New York, he writes a play entitled *Tevye's Daughters*, at whose climax he places the tragic religious confrontation between father and daughter. He rewrites this play twice, returning to this dramatic scene in the various corrections and additions he made to it. He writes of his hesitations and vacillations in a 1914 letter to his wife, as well as discussing the matter with the producers and actors who are to appear on the stage in New York. He originally made Chava voice another explanation for her disappointment and her discovery of the true nature of the situation existing between Christians and Jews. In one version, Chava comes to the home of her sister Bielka who had married a wealthy Jew, whom she tells that she is leaving her Christian husband because he believes that her father needs holy Christian blood for the Passover holiday. Did the Beilis Trial of 1913 impress Shalom Aleikhem with the feeling that, even at the beginning of the twentieth century, Orthodox Russians believed in the anti-Jewish blood libel?

In any event, in the end the author preferred the original version, the one he had written at the outset. Chava returns to her father's house before he leaves it forever, her older sister persuades the father to accept her back because she is his daughter, and the apostate daughter returns to her religion, to her family, and to her people. She returns to Jewishness by admitting that, at the time of her conversion in church she did not listen or relate to what was said and did not accept the basic principles of the religion or of baptism. She returns to her family by declaring that she is her father's daughter as she was before. She returns to her people by sharing in the terrible Jewish experience of exile, loss, and wandering.[2]

At the same time that Shalom Aleikhem was dying of tuberculosis in New York City in 1916 at the age of only fifty-seven, a four-year-old Jewish child was playing in the streets of the Bronx. This child was Joseph Stein, the son of parents who had fled from Poland to America, settled in New York, and established a family. Stein grew up in the Bronx and earned a master's degree in social work. While pursuing his profession, he began to write plays and, in 1948, these began to appear on the Broadway stages. He achieved the height of his fame in 1964 when he reworked the story of Tevye the Milkman into the musical *Fiddler on the Roof*. The title (and backdrop) for this play were taken from Marc Chagall's painting portraying a Jew floating above the earth, playing with great virtuosity on that wonderful musical instrument which it is possible to take everywhere, an instrument that can produce the most melancholy weeping sounds as well as the most joyous tones.

At the end of the musical as reworked by Joseph Stein, when it becomes clear to Tevye that they are being expelled from their town, his daughter Chava appears before him with her Polish Christian husband and tells him that they are leaving, as a couple, to go to the city of Krakow. She then adds a sentence, upon hearing which the audience in the theater begins to applaud: we are unwilling to remain in a place that could do such things to others. Tevye adds, 'God be with you.'

Could Shalom Aleikhem have imagined that a Jew named Joseph Stein would erase the theological debate, the anger against those who abandon their people, and the wonderful insight regarding the inability of the Jew to change his religion—and for all these substitute the new sentence which he placed in Chava's mouth? What would Shalom Aleikhem have thought if he knew that someone would change the climax of this story, into which he had put every fiber of his being, describing the modern Jewish tragedy and the ability of the Jew to rise like a phoenix, specifically in light of their repression by the Christian gentile?

The new Chava does not mention her Jewishness, nor does she leave her husband. She does not return to her people, nor to her religion or to her family. She declares that she belongs to a neutral and universal world of 'good people,' and that she, alongside her loving Christian husband, will set out on their journey together—and specifically to the city of Krakow. This is the manner in which American Jews prefer to resolve the theological confrontation articulated by Shalom Aleikhem one generation earlier.

The question as to how Jews regard one who has abandoned his religion and converted to another lies at the basis of the present study. The timeframe chosen relates to the Jewish confrontation with a changing Christian world in Europe, from the early Middle Ages until the mid-fourteenth century. The method of this research is socio-historical; hence, we have chosen those areas in which the Jews confronted Christians over a lengthy period of time. The study is focused upon France, Germany, and England until the great expulsions from these areas during the course of the fourteenth century (from England in 1290). The Jewry of Christian Spain is deserving of a study in its own right, as it was initially under Muslim rule and only later passed under Christian rule, so that the social structures created there were formed rather differently.

This study began with notes and insights that I received in response to my article published in *Annales* in 1999.[3] All those insights I gained were renewed and expanded with the help of various different researchers who read my paper, and with the help of my students in a course on the subject which I gave every three years in the Department for the History of the Jewish People at Tel Aviv University. My experience regarding both this and other subjects confirms the saying of the Kabbalist R. Shmuel d'Ozidah concerning the concept of *talmidei hakhmamim* (the Hebrew term for scholars; literally, 'student-sage'): 'That it is never justified to call someone a "sage" or "wise man" alone, without adding the term "student"—for if he does not think that he is a student, he is not truly a sage.'[4] I wish to thank all those who commented, criticized, and provided new insights, both researchers and students.

During the years 2005–6 I had the honor of being the guest of Claire Hall College in Cambridge, England. There I began to develop the ideas which are expanded in this research. I enjoyed numerous conversations on the matter of conversion with Miri Rubin as part of the ongoing project, 'Religion and the State in Pre-Modern Europe,' at the Centre for History and Economics in Cambridge. During that time I also took part in two conferences organized by the project which focused on the topic of conversion and which provided additional stimulus for my research. I am grateful for her willingness to answer all my questions, and for the many connections she helped me build with other scholars.

Yitzhak Hen contributed greatly to the quality of this study through his keen criticism and directed me towards much source material and research studies on conversion to Christianity. Yitzhak Lifschitz, with his insights into the halakhic approaches of the medieval scholars, clarified for me many of the complex halakhic issues and sources. Robert Chazan made many constructive comments.

Notes

1 There were twelve stage productions of *Fiddler* in the United States and Great Britain (1964–2007), which received three Tony Awards (Best Musical, Best Score, Best Book), as well a movie version (1971). The film won Academy Awards (for arranger-conductor, best picture, best actor, and best supporting actor).

2 C. Shmeruk, *Studies in Sholem Aleichem's Writings* [Hebrew], ed. C. Turiansky, Jerusalem 2000, pp. 9–32.

3 S. Goldin, 'Juifs et juifs convertis au Moyen Age: 'Es-tu encore mon frére?'' *Annales, Histoire, Sciences Sociales* 54 (1999), pp. 851–874.

4 *Shemuel di Uzidha (Oceda), Midrash Shmu'el*, on *Pirkei Avot*, Bene Berak 1988, beginning of chapter 4; or, in the words of Goethe, 'Bonos vir semper tiro.'

Leading figures

Rabbenu Gershom Meor ha-Golah, Germany 960–1028

Rabbi Shlomo ben Isaac (Rashi) (d. 1105), northern France

Rabbi Eliezer ben Nathan (Ra'avan), Germany 1090–1170

Rabbi Ya'akov ben Meir, Rabbenu Tam, Ramerupt, northern France ca. 1100–71

Rabbi Eliezer ben Yoel ha-Levi (Rabya'h), Germany 1140–1240

Rabbi Eleazar of Worms, Germany 1160–1230

Rabbi Yitzhak ben Moshe of Vienna (Or Zaru'a), 1180–1250

Rabbi Simhah of Speyer (? d. early C.13th)

Rabbi Meir ben Baruch (Maharam of Rothenburg), Germany 1215?–1293

Rabbi Yedidya ben Israel (? d. late C.13th)

Abbreviations

b. Babylonian Talmud

m. Mishnah

t. Tosefta, Moses Samuel Zuckermandel edition, 1888

1

Early beginnings

In a society defined by religion, the attitude towards those who leave it or who wish to join it is one of the fundamentals of self-definition. The attitude of Jews in the Christian world of the Middle Ages towards those Jews who converted to Christianity, or to Christians who sought to join the Jewish religion, reflects the central characteristics of Jewish self-definition as a unique, monotheistic group, chosen by God, which sees itself as fulfilling a particular task in the world.[1] In the present study, we shall examine various aspects of Jewish self-understanding in the context of conversion to another religion—whether it is one of self-confidence or suspicion, of a clear theological position or doubt—as well as confrontation with the problem during the course of the process of socialization. In that way, we can better understand the self-definition of those Jews living as a minority within a Christian majority, whose self-confidence grew steadily between the tenth and the fourteenth century, until this world rejected the Jews completely and expelled them from the countries in which they had lived: England, France, and significant parts of Germany.[2]

The attitude within Jewish society regarding the movement of individuals from Judaism to Christianity, whether as a result of violent necessity (i.e., coercion), or of their own free will, as well as that of Christians into the Jewish religion, is one of the central and most significant issues for understanding the Jewish group during the Middle Ages, and serves as an exciting test case for examining the attitude and behavior of a society under duress.[3] From its earliest days, Christianity perceived itself as the sequel to and heir of Judaism, and as negating the need for it. Moreover, the promise that the Jews would eventually acknowledge the truth of Christianity and become Christians was already embedded in the Christian Scriptures in the words of Paul, 'A remnant shall be saved' (Romans 9:27), creating an ongoing missionary tension between Christians and Jews. In a period during which the ability of a given religion to recruit new adherents from the ranks of the rival religion was seen as a confirmation of its truth, conversion from Judaism to Christianity was understood by Christians as a vindication of the superiority of their faith and of their success in the world. Within Germany and northern France (and, later, of England), from the second half of the tenth century on, we find proof that the Jewish group saw Christianity not only as a theological rival competing with it over the basic principles of religion but as a stubborn and persistent enemy that sought to destroy Judaism. It should be noted here that, from a methodological viewpoint, the current study is concerned with the attitude of one religion towards the intentions of the rival religion towards it—an attitude not necessarily related to the real developments within the other religion during that same period.

In classical Jewish literature (i.e., the Mishnah and the Talmud), which in Palestine encompasses the first centuries of the Christian Era and, in Babylonia, the period from the first through the fifth century, the attitude towards one who had left the Jewish group and those interested in joining it was ambivalent and inconsistent. Those Jews who emulated forms of behavior accepted in the pagan world were referred to as apostates (or *mumarim* in Hebrew), but were not perceived as having completely separated themselves from Judaism; rather, they were seen as continuing to live among Jews, but as having altered some of their behavior in a flagrant and annoying way. During this period, with certain rare exceptions, no one assumed that a Jew who had left his religion and lived as an adherent of a different religion had in fact really lost his Jewish identity.[4]

The concept *mumar* appears in a totally different context in the Mishnah and the Tosefta, related to the prohibition against exchanging or substituting sacrificial animals for one another in the Temple, and what happens if a man or a woman violates that which is explicitly stated in the Torah: 'He shall not substitute anything for it, a good for a bad, or a bad for a good; and if he makes any exchange of beast for beast, then both it and that for which it is exchanged shall be holy' (Leviticus 27:10). Because of the verb used in this verse (ימיר, המר), one who performs such a substitution is called a מומר ('one who substitutes'), and the act is known as substitution (המרה).[5] The concept of *meshumad* (משומד) in the sense of 'apostate' only appears in the Tosefta in the context of a person who does things contrary to the central precepts of the Jewish religion, such as one who eats foods which are forbidden to Jews (e.g., reptiles, insects, carcasses of animals which died by themselves, the flesh of swine, and so forth), drinks wine of pagan libations, desecrates the Sabbath, wears mixed fibers, or 'does those things towards which the Impulse is not inclined.'[6] As against that, the literature of the Talmudic period (third–sixth centuries) mentions dozens of cases in which a new type known as *mumar* or *meshumad* appears: the term *mumar* is taken from the language of exchange or substitution, while the term *meshumad* comes from the verb שמד (shm'd), which, in its original context, seems to have been related to immersion in water, and thereafter acquired the meaning of 'annihilate' or 'destroy.' However, the earlier perception did not change much. The *mumar* is a person who continues to live within the framework of Jewish society, but no longer follows the meticulous observance commanded therein. Rather, he exchanges or substitutes that meticulousness for other practices.

In a lengthy discussion in *Tractate Hullin* (pp. 2–6), it becomes clear that there are different kinds of *mumarim* or *meshumadim*, all of whom continued to live within the Jewish community. For example: there is a *mumar la-'aralot*, who does not wish to have himself circumcised; or a *mumar le-te'avon* (lit., 'a *mumar* for appetite'), defined as one who, when no kosher meat is available, will eat forbidden flesh. There is a distinction drawn between a Jew who is willing to eat the flesh of carcasses or other non-kosher meat only when no kosher meat is available, and one who eats non-kosher meat even when it is possible to eat kosher meat. Even though the former is also called *Yisrael mumar la-nevelot* ('a Jew who violates the law concerning eating non-kosher-slaughtered meat'), the attitude towards him is the same as that towards any other regular Jew. Thus, for example, one is obligated to redeem him should he fall into captivity, and meat which he slaughters is considered kosher. The *amoraim* Ravva (first half of the fourth century) and Rav Ashi (about a hundred years later), explained that when such a person is confronted with that which is permitted and with that which is prohibited—e.g., kosher meat and non-kosher meat—he will always prefer the former; only insofar as no kosher food is available will he eat non-kosher.[7] The more extreme type, known as *mumar le-hakh'is* ('an apostate out of spite') or *mumar le-kol ha-Torah kulah* ('one who denies the entire Torah')—that is to say, one who deliberately violates those religious laws which every Jew observes—is classified in a harsher and more distancing manner. However, it is implied by the discussion that he too continues to live within the Jewish collectivity and maintains a similar way of life to that of his erstwhile fellows, as before.[8] This approach is expressed in a Talmudic passage concerning the *'eruv*. The *'eruv* is the method by which people living around a common courtyard may ease certain of the Sabbath restrictions somewhat. It is clear that such halakhic cooperation is only possible among those who are Jews and to whom the laws of the Sabbath apply. From this discussion, it becomes clear that *mumarim* participated in the *'eruv*, and that some also observed the Sabbath.[9] The discussion revolves around various definitions of *mumar* and his attitude towards the Sabbath. There are those who violate the Sabbath in private, but publicly observe the Sabbath, while there are others who are literally 'apostates to idolatry'—but all of them live within the Jewish neighborhood in one of the apartments among all of the Jews in the shared courtyard.

The harshest definition is that of 'an apostate to the entire Torah' (משומד לכל התורה כולה), defined as one from whom one does not accept a sacrifice and to whom there is applied the well-known verse, 'When a person offers from among you' (Leviticus 1:2)—and its interpretation, 'for among you I have separated it and not from among the nations.' That is to say: we see him as being numbered 'among the nations' and not as part of the people of Israel; or, to use the language of the Talmud, 'From this we conclude: one accepts sacrifices from among the sinners of Israel so that they may return as penitents, apart from the *meshumad* and one who pours out pagan libations and desecrates the Sabbath publicly.'[10]

Those who wished to join Judaism were received with a degree of suspicion as to their motivations, but a certain process and ceremonies were created by which they could be accepted into Judaism.[11] At the basis of the Jewish theological perception lay the assumption that Jews were the descendants of those who had made an eternal covenant with God at Mount Sinai at the time of receiving the Torah. Whoever is among the offspring of those people is seen as a Jew in his essence, and nothing can change this. Whoever wishes to join the Jewish people and is not numbered among the descendants of those who made the covenant may join them, but must 'organize' a special status for himself. The literature written during the first centuries CE contains various suggestions as to how to organize such transition into the new religion.

The fact that classical Jewish literature was often ambivalent and inconsistent in its attitude towards Jewish converts to Christianity was deeply rooted in the circumstances surrounding the development of Christianity in the first few centuries of its existence. Indeed, the Jewish attitude towards converts to Christianity differed depending on the historical period in which it arose: as a new and persecuted religion until the fourth century; as the religion of the empire, but subject to the grip of rulers and emperors until the eleventh century; and during the subsequent era, as it became a religion that influenced rulers and was dominant organizationally, politically, and theologically throughout Europe, one that was victorious over Islam and that established the Crusader Kingdom of Jerusalem. During each of these stages, the attitude of Judaism towards those who converted to the rival religion was a clear indication of its own self-perception and identity. The Jews were familiar with the view that Christianity was the heir of Judaism and that it was the intention of Christians to convert the Jews to their faith at every possible opportunity. And indeed, those who fashioned the Christian religion—theologians, members of the ecclesiastical hierarchy (bishops, archbishops, popes, and monks), as well as the simple people—were given the opportunity to act. Hence, the Jews' resistance to Christian missionary efforts became one of the cornerstones shaping their identity as a group.

Between the fifth and tenth centuries almost all of the groups in central and Western Europe took shape as Christian ones, constructing their own identity within the framework of the victorious and dominant religion. They were insistent upon language, forms of warfare, forms of dress, ancient customs, etc.[12] The question that needs to be asked is why, between the fifth and the tenth centuries, did Christian society by and large refrain from applying ongoing, violent pressure upon the Jews to change their religion, while making every effort to convert the pagan inhabitants of Europe to the Christian religion? In order to resolve this puzzle, scholars have noted a theological factor which underlies this—namely, Augustine's doctrine of witness.[13] However, a deeper examination of the complaints of the bishops of Lyon during the ninth century reveals that what protected the Jews from missionary domination was not a theological reason but rather the rulers' perception of their own interests, and especially the Jews' own unwillingness to convert.[14]

The Jews as a group first appear in the German cultural sphere during the course of the ninth century, as a result of the rulers' invitation to the Jews to settle as merchants in the cities of Germany, which were predominantly located upon rivers. Following negotiation with the rulers, these merchants settled with their families. There are extant documents of *privilege* granted to the Jews as early as the reign of Emperor Louis the Pious between 814 and 825, and thereafter, during the period of the emperors Otto. Otto I (962–73), and Otto II (973–83), developed the cities along the length of the River Rhine, placing at their heads bishops whom they made branches of their rule.[15] Thus, by the end of the eleventh century, Magdeburg and Merseburg on the Elbe, Mainz, Cologne, Worms, and Speyer on the Rhine, Trier on the Moselle, Prague on the Vitava, Bamberg on the Main, and Regensburg on the Danube became trade cities that encouraged Jewish settlement.[16] Immediately upon their arrival, these merchants demanded and received an order from the emperor Louis the Pious, strictly forbidding Christians to persuade the pagan servants of the Jews to be baptized as Christians, an act which would have freed them from servitude. By this measure they determined, in concert with the emperor, that Christian missionizing had no obligatory force over them in those places where they lived. Against this background, tension was created between Agobard, the bishop of Lyon, and his successor Amolo against the emperor. Agobard speaks of the preferred status of the Jews, of their arrogance, of their attacking a Jewish woman who had converted to Christianity, and of their attempts to persuade Christians to convert to Judaism. Agobard's claim against him was that, as a Christian emperor he ought not to permit such improper behavior on the part of the Jews. Agobard was concerned about the influence of the Jews on the Christians and upon the pagan servants of the Jews, among whom there was nobody who was really interested in converting to Christianity. Agobard's successor to the bishopric of Lyon, Amolo (841–52), served during the period of the conversion to Judaism of the emperor's deacon, Bodo (Eleazar), and was more extreme than his predecessor in his attacks.[17] The fear of Christian conversion to Judaism, supported by rumors of senior churchmen who had converted, added a hysterical note to these suspicions. During the course of the eleventh century, we hear of several church notables who converted to Judaism and fled from Christian lands in order to live openly as Jews and to attack their former religion: Wecelinus, early in the eleventh century, Andreas, the archbishop of Bariin 1098, and Obadiah, the Norman convert at the beginning of the twelfth century.[18] The fact that these churchmen converted to Judaism of their own free will and from inner conviction was in stark opposition to the activities of the Church at that time, which were intended to convert Jews to Christianity against their will. The Christian demand for conversion to Christianity was accompanied by threats to their lives: the Christians were not interested in the inner world of the apostate or whether he was really interested in becoming a Christian. The bishop of Limoges threatened the Jewish community that it either convert to Christianity or leave. After a month of polemics, only three or four Jews agreed to do so, while all the rest left. Similarly, the Christian need to portray Jews who converted to Christianity as being the result of extraordinary miracles was rooted in the weakness of Christian theological arguments. The Jew who converted to Christianity was not convinced spiritually or in terms of faith but rather by the shock that hit him upon seeing a miraculous change in nature.[19]

Jewish sources from the tenth century until after the First Crusade (i.e., beginning of twelfth century) do not conceal the fact that there were Jews who converted to Christianity—some under coercion but some willingly—who became real Christians. These Jews were seen as deviant; nevertheless, the tendency of the Jewish leadership was not to sacrifice them to the rival religion but to emphasize that the way to return to Judaism remained open to them. From their point of view, allowing these Jews to return to Judaism strengthened that approach which saw Judaism as a victorious religion, which did not give up on those who converted to the rival religion. The desire not to forego even a single Jew who had gone astray derives, on the one hand, from an impressive degree of confidence in the power of the Jewish religion but, on the other hand, from a basic sense of contempt regarding the persuasive powers of Christianity. It is known that two central personalities in German Jewry at the turn of the tenth century had children who converted to Christianity. Rabbi Shimon ben Yitzhak ben Abun (950?–1020?) was the greatest religious poet of his time, and his son Elhanan converted to Christianity. Rabbenu Gershom ben Yehudah (Meor ha-Golah, 960–1028), was the leading halakhic authority at the end of the tenth and beginning of the eleventh century, and his son likewise converted. These two young people converted to Christianity willingly, not as the result of coercion. Early sources report that when Rabbenu Gershom's son died he observed a double mourning period of *shivah* for him, and that Rabbi Shimon tried to bring his son back (to Judaism) through the rulers. Beyond that, nothing is mentioned of this. Centuries would pass before these two 'heroes' would be considered in a different manner.[20]

Rabbenu Gershom related extensively in his writings to Christianity and to its dangers. His theological approach to Christianity and to its converts may be found both in his halakhic writings and in his poetic-liturgical writing (called in Hebrew *piyyutim*).[21] Rabbenu Gershom Meor ha-Golah wrote *piyyutim*, primarily of the genre of *Selihot*.[22] These *piyyutim*, beyond being part of a ritual liturgical framework, served a double function: they include clearly identifiable theological polemics intended for internal purposes, to strengthen the Jews against the difficulties of life, the attacks by Christians, and feelings of despair; but they also contain passages addressed directly to Jewish converts to Christianity, propaganda aimed at those who had abandoned Judaism and were within Christianity, appealing to them to return. Rabbenu Gershom describes the pressure to which these Jews are subjected on the part of the Christians, the lack of hope stemming from the lengthy period of time that had elapsed since the beginning of the Exile, and the failure of the long-promised Divine redemption to manifest itself. His *piyyutim* contain harsh descriptions of Christianity as a vile, pernicious religion which seeks to convert Jews into Christians, representing the miserable situation of the Jews as proof of the falsehood of their belief. He refers to Christianity as 'impure,' 'dead,' 'newly arrived,' and anticipates its destruction, while simultaneously awaiting the moment when the entire world will recognize the Jewish God as the God of the World and His ability to redeem His people.[23]

Alongside the attacks against Christianity, Rabbenu Gershom fashioned propaganda intended to strengthen Jews against the theological temptations to convert to Christianity, as well as referring to those who had already converted as vacillating, recognizing their potential to return to Judaism permanently. In other words, he labeled the converts to Christianity as individuals who were not really convinced of their new religion and would soon return to Judaism. Thus, his propaganda worked both to convince those who had abandoned Judaism and at the same time to strengthen those who remained Jews, emphasizing the imminent return of the converts to Christianity. The question must be asked: did Rabbenu Gershom really assume or at least hope that the Jews who had converted would read the *piyyutim* he had written, or did he address them as a kind of rhetorical exercise intended primarily for his Jewish readers? In my opinion, as shall be clarified below, it was the accepted view among Jewish authors until the middle of the thirteenth century that the converts to Christianity were aware of what Jews were writing, knew what was going on in their former society, and were open to its influence.

In one of Rabbenu Gershom's liturgical poems, *Eilekha niqra* ('We call to You'), one can see the use of this mechanism as a sophisticated means of addressing those who had already accepted Christianity out of despair, fear, or theological acceptance. The *piyyut* begins by calling upon God and depicting the new 'trouble' caused by the 'pernicious' Christians, who lay against the Jews 'an evil plot'—namely, to convert them to Christianity. His description of the Christian god serves simultaneously as a contemptuous portrait, intended to show loyal Jews the temptations of Christianity as a pagan religion, as well as a protest against those who had been convinced by fear or despair and were now Christians. It may even have been addressed to his son, whom Rabbenu Gershom asks to reflect upon his acts: Who is your God? 'To accept as God the contemptuous sadness / bowing before a symbol / an image and worshipping before him / and to an unholy thing [as if] he greatly forgives / nor to fear the awesome God.'[24] He reminds the apostates that they ought not forget or abandon the eternal God of their fathers in favor of 'one who is impure and dead, new and recently come.'

Rabbenu Gershom alludes, on the one hand, to those who serve God and are His pious ones and, on the other, to the traitors and rebels: 'Turn, O Lord, to the prayer of Your servants / redeem and deliver them from those who betray You / Command the salvation of the seed of Your pious ones / take [them] out to relief from the din of those who rebel against You.'[25] It is clear that this *Selihah* deals directly with those who converted to Christianity—'who betray You'—and with those who remain Jews despite everything ('Your pious ones'). He emphasizes that the problematic points of his people at this juncture are their 'powerlessness' and that 'money is gone from the pockets'—that is, despair and economic blows.[26] He asks God to suppress the Quality of Judgment and to bring closer the Quality of Mercy, for He has not given up on those who converted to Christianity. It would appear that Rabbenu Gershom imagined that those who converted to Christianity, who were now Christians, were nevertheless prepared to hear the voice of reason, the voice of Judaism, and that he had not yet despaired of them even after they had taken the radical step of converting to the new religion. He also informs them that their repentance will be accepted by God. In his *piyyutim*, Rabbenu Gershom notes the connection between the threat of expelling the Jews from Christian cities and their conversion. We know of the expulsion of Jews from Mainz in 1012 by the emperor Henry II. It is possible that some Jews converted in order to avoid this expulsion, Rabbenu Gershom's son among them.[27] We cannot know whether he had in mind his son, who converted to Christianity and died as a Christian, when he wrote this poem. It is nevertheless clear that he was the man before whom the way back to Judaism ought not to be blocked.[28]

In terms of the halakhic perspective, Rabbenu Gershom defined the converts to Christianity as 'apostates'; however, he wrote a halakhic decision stating that their acts were done as a temporary error, and that therefore one must assure that the gates of return to Judaism are not closed to them, as they shall return to Judaism in the future. Nevertheless, he was clearly aware that the Jewish community did not accept his view of the apostates as self-evident, and that there was suspicion and fear of those apostates who returned to Judaism. Such a protest is evident from two questions that were addressed to Rabbenu Gershom regarding *kohanim* (members of the hereditary priesthood) who had converted to Christianity and returned to Judaism and wished to return to their traditional role in the synagogue: to be called to the Torah first and to bless the people with the Priestly Blessing on festival days.[29] From the questions addressed to him, it is clear that the public did not see such a decision in a positive light, and there were those who opposed it on the basis of the claim that conversion to another religion nullified the privilege given to this person from birth, and that now that he has returned he is no longer considered the same person. In other words, they assumed that something in the essence of the person changed when he converted to Christianity.

This argument is worthwhile giving our attention to: the assumption is that, from now on, the definition of the Jew was of a person who was without blemish. The convert to Christianity who returns to Judaism is blemished, even if he regrets what he had done. The justification for this view is based upon a verse in the Torah: it is written that God will give the priests the ability to bless the people, 'And they shall place my name upon the children of Israel, and I will bless them' (Numbers 6:27). That is to say, the priests bless because God agrees that they should do so; in effect, He blesses through them. The *kohen* who converted to Christianity and left Jewry is also abandoned by God (here interpreting the verse, 'And they shall abandon Me and break My covenant'; Deuteronomy 31:16). It is not reasonable that such a person, even if he returns to Judaism, serves as a channel for God's blessing of His people. Rabbenu Gershom Meor ha-Golah, and in his wake all the Rabbinic leaders of the eleventh century, attempted to correct this public impression, refuting this argument with halakhic reasons that would be convincing to the people. An analogy was drawn to a priest who suffered a physical blemish who, though not permitted to offer sacrifices in the Temple, is nevertheless allowed to bless the people. Moreover, everything is forgiven to one who has repented. Rabbenu Gershom presented two rhetorical arguments of significant weight: first, he states that, from an ethical viewpoint, one of the most serious sins is 'oppressing another through words.'[30] One who prevents a *kohen* from going up to say the blessing and tells him that this is because he had been a Christian insults him and causes him grave emotional pain. Moreover, from a practical viewpoint, adds Rabbenu Gershom, 'you weaken their hand' (a quotation from *b. Sanhedrin* 103a); that is, according to his approach one ought to encourage those who returned to Judaism, so that other apostates will understand that it is worthwhile to do so. Yet notwithstanding Rabbenu Gershom's efforts to reinstate to his original, pre-conversion status one who had become a Christian and now returned to Judaism, he was only partly successful. He was pressured to draw a distinction between a *kohen* who was forced to convert to Christianity and subsequently returned, who was permitted to return to his priestly function, and one who converted of his own free will, who was forbidden to bless the people and, according to some, was also barred from receiving the first *aliyah* to the Torah.[31] Moreover, a *kohen* who had converted to

Christianity and become a Christian preacher or even a monk—'a teacher of idolatry, and this was his function'—clearly lost his priestly status. Even if he repented and returned to Judaism, he cannot bless the people.[32] But despite all these efforts, the popular perception tended to see conversion to Christianity in a very negative light, and remained suspicious of the 'apostate' who returned to Judaism. In order to impose his decision, Rabbenu Gershom introduced an edict prohibiting any harm being done to those who had been Christians (whether converted by force or of their own free will) and returned to Judaism. In this edict, it is forbidden for members of the community to remind them of their past as Christians, they may not refer to them as 'apostates,' nor say that 'they had been immersed in the waters of apostasy' (i.e., the baptismal waters). Rabbenu Gershom was troubled by the fact that, due to the suspicion, shame, and insults that would henceforth be the lot of Jews who had gone astray, they would refrain from returning to Judaism, 'Since one must not weaken the hands of penitents, and it is not correct to do so ... lest they say, "Woe because of that shame, woe to that disgrace," and refrain from returning.' It is emphasized here that this prohibition likewise includes proselytes to Judaism—i.e., that one is not allowed to mention their Christian past. For the first time, one finds a similar attitude applied to an apostate who had returned to Judaism and to a Christian who had converted—an issue to which we shall return further on. It is not clear to what extent this edict was applied in actuality. Two generations after Rabbenu Gershom, during the course of a dispute between two families, one of the sides referred to the other as having been 'immersed in the waters of apostasy.' It was necessary to remind them that Rabbenu Gershom had long since introduced an edict according to which one who mentioned a former apostate's past was in a state of *nidduy* (banned from the community).[33]

Nevertheless, Rabbenu Gershom drew a clear distinction between a Jew who remained a Jew and one who was now a Christian. In response to a question concerning the inheritance of an apostate, Rabbenu Gershom states that one who converted to Christianity could not inherit his father's property. It should be emphasized that he learned this approach 'from Heaven,' in a responsum which was unchallenged.[34]

In addition to the ruling that he had received from Heaven, Rabbenu Gershom marshaled to his assistance God's words to Abraham in the Book of Genesis. At the beginning of God's revelation to Abraham in Chapter 17, God says: 'And I will establish my covenant between me and you and your descendants after you throughout the generations for an everlasting covenant, to be God to you and your descendants after you. And I will give to you, and to your descendants after you, the land of your sojourning, all the land of Canaan, for an everlasting possession; and I will be their God' (Genesis 17:7–8). Similarly, in the Covenant between the Pieces God says: 'On that day the Lord made a covenant with Abram, saying, "To your descendants I give this land, from the river of Egypt to the great river, the River Euphrates"' (Genesis 15:18). From the definitive emphasis on the word 'your descendants' (*zar'akha*), one may conclude that the inheritance only passes to one whose descendants are in fact considered as such. Hence the apostate, whose offspring are not considered as his descendants, is not considered to be related to his father and does not inherit from him. How do we know this? Abraham had two sons, Isaac and Ishmael; nevertheless, Ishmael does not share in the inheritance of those lands—Canaan and others—concerning which God said to Abraham, 'I will give it to you.' This implies that Ishmael is not considered the seed of Abraham and does not share in his inheritance. The same rule applies to subsequent generations. God said to Isaac: 'For to you and to your descendants I will give all these lands' (Genesis 26:3). Isaac also had two sons, Jacob and Esau, and Esau did not inherit Isaac's possession; rather, 'Esau dwelt in the hill country of Seir' (Genesis 36:8), an area outside of the land of Canaan. By contrast, concerning the children of Jacob it is written: 'And I will bring you into the land which I swore to give to Abraham, to Isaac, and to Jacob' (Exodus 6:8). The Land of Israel was given to the sons of Jacob as an inheritance, but not to the children of Esau. Even when God portrays to Abraham the destiny of his offspring, using the words 'your descendants,' the descent into Egypt is conceived of as paying off a debt, in exchange for which they inherit the Land of Israel which relates to the 'seed' of the children of Jacob alone, and not to that of Esau ('Know of a surety that your descendants will be sojourners': Genesis 15:13). From all this, one may conclude that only one perceived as descended from his father is considered his descendant. The apostate is thus considered as belonging to another people, and does not inherit from his father, not being considered as his son.

Rabbenu Gershom is well aware that the Talmudic discussion explicitly states that a person who is not Jewish inherits from his father (*b. Kiddushin* 18a). However, he takes pains in his writing to emphasize that the *meshumad* is not considered a Gentile. A Gentile indeed inherits from his father according to Torah law; thus we find that the sons of Esau inherited their father Esau, as is stated: 'For as an inheritance for Esau because I have given Mount Seir to Esau as a possession' (Deuteronomy 2:5), but Esau did not inherit from Isaac, as Mount Seir does not belong to Isaac but to Esau, as is stated, 'And I gave Esau the hill-country of Seir to possess' (Joshua 24:4).

From this we may conclude that an apostate does not inherit from his father. In other words, Rabbenu Gershom completely nullifies here the autonomous identity of the convert to Christianity. He does not see the apostate as inheriting from his Jewish father, as by his act he forfeited belonging to his father's offspring. Nor does he see him as a 'non-Jew,' as an ordinary Gentile. Rather, Rabbenu Gershom represents him as an individual with a nebulous identity, floating in a kind of limbo based upon nothing.

The apostate who has become a Christian has become part of 'another people' and lost the quality of being the 'seed' of his own people. Nevertheless, the door is always open for him to return to Judaism. And indeed, Rabbenu Gershom's disciple, Rabbi Yehudah, refers to the convert to Christianity as *muhlaf* ('one who has been exchanged').[35]

During the second half of the eleventh century it became clear that there was a need to follow a clear policy pertaining to a 'character' of that sort who deviates from the way of the group in such a flagrant manner. This was done by Rashi, Rabbi Shlomo Yitzhaki, in northern France. Similar to Rabbenu Gershom two generations before him, Rashi defined the Jewish group in terms sharply delineated against the Christian world. Rashi sees Jewish identity as a firm rock which serves as the basis of the faith, and finds it difficult to see a Jew as actually changing his religion to Christianity, thereby harming the Jewish ability to prove its eternity against the Christian religion. Rashi prefers to use the term 'brotherhood.' He sees the convert to Christianity as a Jew who has been forced to deny his religion, or as one whose conversion is the result of a temporary error.[36] Hence, he is fervently opposed to any decision which would cut off the convert to Christianity from his Jewish roots. It was he who determined that the state of brotherhood binding all Jews does not cease even if a person decides to change his religion; all the more so if he was forced to convert to another religion.[37]

Rashi's decision, leaving one who has converted to Christianity as a 'brother' within the Jewish people despite his apostasy, raised substantive problems. Analysis of this will clarify Rashi's far-reaching position:[38] namely, that the essential relationship of a Jew to other Jews is one of 'brotherhood'; hence, there applies to him the principle invoked by Rashi: 'An Israelite, [even though] he has sinned—is [nevertheless] an Israelite.' If he has sinned, his essence remains Jewish; thus, even if he converted to another religion, the rules that apply to every Jew apply to him as well. Therefore, his wife may only be released from marriage to him through the 'Jewish manner' of divorce—that is, by him giving her a *get,* a Jewish divorce writ.[39] When Rashi confronted a question involving a widow who required *halitzah* from her late husband's brother who had converted, he insisted that the woman be freed by means of *halitzah* from the apostate, who was now a Christian—thereby determining that the Jewish essence of the convert to Christianity remained as it was.[40] Rashi does not attempt to classify the convert to Christianity as being 'dead' from the viewpoint of Judaism, and hence as if not existing at all (as their counterparts are defined in other religions), nor was he tempted by a solution proposed in the Geonic literature, according to which if the brother converted to Christianity before the couple had married it was as if he no longer existed and the widow was free because her late husband had no brother. Rashi was shocked by such a solution. The essence of the Jew does not change; hence, the question as to when the brother converted in relation to the time of the marriage is of no significance:

> A woman whose husband dies and they have no sons and his brother is a *meshumad* (converted to Christianity) requires *halitzah*. In order to free herself and remarry, she must make sure that the Christian 'brother' performs the *halitzah* ceremony. It does not matter if the brother became a Christian before or after the wedding ceremony of his brother, as the Jew who converts remains a Jew, as it is written in the Talmud in *Tractate Sanhedrin*, 'A son of Israel who sins is still Israel.' Rabbi Abba b. Zabda said: 'Even though [the people] have sinned, they are still [called] Israel,' and he may not be removed from the Religion of Israel, albeit he cannot be relied upon to testify in matters of prohibitions, or (other) issues related to religious matters. His wine is *yayin nesekh* (libation wine) as he is apparently an idolator, but the marriage that he undertakes remains valid, and he has the ability to perform *yibbum* (levirate marriage) or *halitzah*. The responsum found in the writings of the Geonim, i.e., that the time of the conversion needs to be investigated in relation to the marriage of his brother, should not be relied upon, as it entails an internal contradiction; namely, if his link to Judaism remains as it was, and his ability to perform *halitzah* remains as it was after his conversion, what difference does it make when he converted in relation to his brother's marriage? The answer is that, in order for the woman to be released and free to remarry, the brother must release her through *halitzah*.[41]

In another responsum, Rashi writes that it is forbidden to take interest from a Jew who has converted to Christianity because the assumption that he is a brother remains valid even if he converts and sins, as it is written: 'A Jew who sins, even though he has sinned, remains a Jew.' From the viewpoint of the requirement for a *get* and *halitzah* (i.e., matters of marriage and divorce), he remains a Jew like any other Jew. If he tries to commit a fraud by sending someone in his place, and it is discovered afterwards that the pledge was his, he may be charged interest.[42] The logic behind this is clear. The appropriate thing to do is not to block the way of converts to Christianity to return to Judaism. Were they to be declared lost to Judaism, and their wives allowed to remarry as if they were widows, and if they are considered Christians from the economic point of view, then they will never want to return to their religion.

On the basis of this reasoning, Rashi permitted the Jewish heirs of one who had converted to Christianity to inherit property that had been left with another Jew as a pledge (e.g., as security for a loan or some other obligation).[43] Even if the Jew in question defines himself at present not as a Jew but as a Christian, his essence has not changed. If there is a 'pledge' which he has left with a Jew, then this property may in principle be passed on to his heirs (after his death). True, Rashi describes the apostate as an 'evildoer,' but just as the Torah does not prevent evildoers from inheriting property (the example given is that of Esau!), there is nothing to prevent the relatives of a convert, who remain Jews, to inherit his property. In the event that the relatives of the apostate who died sue the person with whom he had entrusted his property while living as a Christian, their property is to be returned to them. Moreover, Rashi emphasizes that if the guardian of the property appropriated to himself that which the apostate had left with him, he is considered a thief—although in this case, says Rashi, the Rabbinic Court is unable to intervene. This responsum teaches us a great deal about the way of life of the 'apostate' in Rashi's day. He maintains proximity both to the Jewish community and to his relatives who remained Jews. The Jew holding the pledge of the new Christian succeeded in dealing with him and did not return it until the latter died, at which time he passed it on to those of his relatives who remained Jews. Rashi, who here represents the Rabbinic judges, explains that because the owner of the pledge is still considered as a Jew in terms of his essence, there is no doubt that he was entitled to receive his pledge back but, he emphasizes, 'the judges have no power to remove it from him'—that is, he does not activate the Rabbinic Court to assist the apostate. This is evidently so because, even though he sees the Jewish 'essence' within him, in terms of everyday matters he is at present a Christian. Notwithstanding this, Rashi emphasizes that the children born to the apostate while he was a Christian are not considered his heirs; thus, upon his death the pledge returns to his true heirs, his Jewish relatives, and not to his Christian children.

In his comments concerning the inheritance of the apostate, Rashi continues his approach according to which a Jew who has converted to Christianity is denied his patrimony. This approach already existed in the previous period. At the beginning of the Middle Ages the Christians took note of the fact that the Jews denied converts to Christianity their inheritance with the help of their parents' will, thereby creating a situation in which they became a burden upon the Christian community. Already in the fifth century Christian legislation attempted to nullify this possibility. Hence, the emperors Theodosius II and Valentinianus III, in legislation from 426, stated that a will aimed to deprive a convert to Christianity of his inheritance or to bypass him is null and void; if such a will is in fact made, it is treated as if it had never been written and the (Christian) heir inherits as if there were no will.[44] Notwithstanding this legislation, Rashi's words seem to have been intended to negate the possibility that his words regarding the 'objective Jewishness' of the convert might be understood as implying that he would also receive his patrimony. According to Rashi, the apostate's principled or theoretical Jewishness does not alter the fact that he became a Christian of his own free will, and as such was not fit to inherit from his ancestors as a Jew. His property will be kept against the possibility that he might recant his conversion, or for the benefit of those members of his family who remained Jewish.

A certain Rabbinic Court addressed Rashi with a question concerning those Jews who had been forced to convert to Christianity who had returned to Judaism. The judges asked his opinion as to whether one could accept testimony from people who were Christians at the time of the event in question and testified to what they saw as Christians. Rashi answers that it depends upon the nature of their behavior at the time that Christianity was imposed upon them. If the Rabbinic Court, upon clarifying the matter, arrives at the conclusion that they secretly practiced the Jewish religion while they were Christians and did no more than what the Christians forced them to do, their testimony is acceptable. 'If,' on the other hand, 'they were guilty of performing transgressions which were not imposed upon them by the Gentiles,' one should not accept their testimony.[45] This decision by Rashi is not self-evident. A witness must be an honest and upright person; thus, it is impossible for a person defined by the Talmud as an 'evildoer' to be a witness. The definitions in the Talmud indicate that one who is an 'apostate' is an evildoer; hence, he is clearly unfit for testimony.[46] The fact that Rashi instructs the Rabbinic Court to examine the actions of these apostates at the time that they were Christians redefines them as Jews and not as the 'apostates' as found in the Talmud. That is,

Rashi understands a Jew who converted to Christianity under duress to be a Jew in every sense. If he was considered 'wicked,' then he would be unable to testify as to what he saw—not because he is not a Jew, but because he is a 'wicked Jew,' and as such unfit for testimony. Thus, even if he repented for having been a Christian, at the time that he saw what happened he was an 'evildoer' and, according to Rashi, is unable to give testimony. Hence, if an apostate Jew married a woman, and both she and all the witnesses were forced converts, the marriage is valid, and if they wish to divorce he must give her a Jewish divorce writ. All of these 'Christianizers' are considered as Jews because 'An Israelite who sins—is nevertheless an Israelite'; moreover, these people did so under coercion and 'their hearts were directed to Heaven.' Thus, everything they did was valid, and they are able to testify as to what they saw.[47] Already at this stage we can see that, while the popular mind regarded conversion from Judaism to Christianity in a negative light, suspecting their motivations both at the time they converted and when they returned to Judaism, those who determined the approach of Rabbinic Judaism preferred to see those who converted to Christianity as forced converts, or as individuals acting under temporary error, and made efforts to return them to Judaism at all costs.

Notes

1 Both phenomena—that of leaving Jewish society and religion in favor of Christian society and religion and its opposite—continued for the entire period; however, they are reflected very differently in the written sources. Conversion to Christianity being a central problem with which Jewish society dealt, there are numerous and varied sources on this issue. The subject is discussed in chronicle literature, in halakhic literature, in the responsa literature in light of the numerous questions and problems which were elicited by this new situation, in liturgical poetry (*piyyutim*), in inter-religious polemics, and elsewhere. Those who joined Judaism were a minority who endangered both themselves and the community, hence references to them are extremely sparse and concealed in various guises.

2 Spain was an exception, as a monarchy in which the Jews found themselves between two rival religions that were struggling with one another, hence, we shall not treat it in this study. This aspect of the self-definition of Jews who write about those who became Christians will be useful for a number of issues discussed by the historians of the end of the Middle Ages and the beginning of the modern era. See e.g., E. Fram, 'Perception and Reception of Repentant Apostates in Medieval Ashkenaz and Premodern Poland,' *Association for Jewish Studies Review* 21 (1996), pp. 299–339; E. Carlebach, *Divided Soul*, New Haven 2001.

3 The literature about Christianizing Jews in the Middle Ages is extremely
   extensive. See: J. Aronius, *Regesten zur Geschichte der Juden im frankischen
   und deutschen Reiche bis zum Jahre 1273*, Berlin 1902, Nos. 102, 204, 223,
   771; P. Browe, *Die Judenmission im Mittelalter und die Päpste*, Rome 1942;
   B. Blumenkranz, 'Jüdische und Christliche Konvertiten im jüdisch-christlichen Religions gespräch des Mittelalters,' in: *Judentum im Mittelalter: Beiträge
   zum christlich-jüdischen Gespräch*, ed. P. Wilpert, Berlin 1966, pp. 264–283;
   S. Grayzel, *The Church and the Jews in the XIIIth Century*, rev. edition, New York
   1966, p. 296; J. Katz, 'Even Though a Sinner, He is Still of Israel' [Hebrew]
   Tarbiz 27 (1958), pp. 203–227; J. Katz, *Exclusiveness and Tolerance*, Oxford 1961;
   S. Grayzel, 'Popes, Jews, and Inquisition: from "Sicu" to "Torbato corde,"' in:
   Essays on the Occasion of the Seventieth Anniversary of Dropsie University (1909–1979),
   eds. A. Katsch and L. Nemoy, Philadelphia 1977, pp. 151–188; Philippe de
   Villepreux in F. J. Pegues, *The Lawyers of the Last Capetians*, Princeton 1962,
   pp. 124–140; G. J. Blidstein, 'Who is not a Jew? The Medieval Discussion,'
   Israel Law Review 11 (1976), pp. 369–390; R. Chazan, *European Jewry and the
   First Crusade*, Berkely 1987, pp. 146–147; W. C. Jordan, *The French Monarchy
   and the Jews: From Philip Augustus to the Last Capetians*, Philadelphia 1989, pp. 89,
   138–139, 149–150; W. J. Pakter, *Medieval Canon Law and the Jews*, Ebelsbach
   am Main 1988, pp. 315–317, Nos. 265, 269–275; S. Simonsohn, *The Apostolic
   See and the Jews*, Toronto 1991, pp. 238–262; R. C. Stacey, 'The Conversion
   of Jews to Christianity in Thirteenth-Century England,' *Speculum* 67 (1992),
   pp. 263–283; S. Goldin, 'Juifs et juifs convertis au Moyen Age: "Es-tu encore
   mon frére?,"' *Annales, Histoire, Sciences Sociales* 54 (1999), pp. 851–874;
   A. Haverkamp, 'Baptised Jews in German Lands during the Twelfth Century,'
   in: *Jews and Christians in Twelfth-Century Europe*, eds. M. A. Signer and J. Van
   Engen, Notre Dame, Ind. 2001, pp. 255–310; M. Perry, *Tradition and Transformation: Knowledge Transmission among European Jews in the Middle Ages*, Tel Aviv
   2010, pp. 115–194.

4 O. Irshai, 'The Apostate as an Inheritor in Geonic Responsa: Basics of
   Decision Making and Parallels in Gentile Law,' *Shenaton ha-Mishpat ha-Ivri*
   11–12 (1984–86), pp. 435–462.

5 *m. Temurah* 1.1.

6 *t. Horayot* 1.5; *t. Hullin* 1.1; *t. Demai* 2.4.

7 *b. Hullin* 2a–6b; *Gittin* 47a. (*Amoraim*: Sages in the time of the Talmud.)

8 *b. Sanhedrin* 27a; *Avodah Zarah* 26b.

9 *b. Eruvin* 659a–b.

10 *b. Eruvin* 69b; *Hullin* 13b, 41a; *Horayot* 8a; *Avodah Zarah* 64b.

11 In his book, Gary Porton calls them *The Stranger Within Your Gates*, Chicago
   1994; see especially his conclusions, pp. 193–220.

12 W. Pohl, 'Telling the Difference: Signs of Ethnic Identity,' in: *Strategies of
   Distinction: The Contracting of Ethnic Communities, 300–900*, ed. W. Pohl with
   H. Reimitz, Leiden 1998, pp. 17–69.

13 J. Cohen, '"Slay them not": Augustine and the Jews in Modern Scholarship,' *Medieval Encounters* 4 (1998), pp. 78–92.

14 Simonsohn, *The Apostolic See and the Jews*, pp. 94–100; J. Heil, 'Agobard, Amolo, das Kirchengut und die Juden von Lyon,' *Francia* 25 (1998), pp. 39–76.

15 See E. Boshof, *Königtum und Königschersschaft im 10 und 11 Jahrhundert*, Munich 1993, pp. 10–23; E. Müller-Mertens, 'The Ottonians as Kings and Emperors,' in: *The New Cambridge Medieval History*, Vol. 3, ed. T. Reuter, Cambridge 1999, pp. 233–266 (esp. pp. 254–260).

16 *Germania Judaica*, eds. I. Elbogen, A. Freimann, and H. Tykocinski, Vol. 1, Tübingen 1963: Magdeburg (pp. 163–164), Merseburg (226–228), Mainz (174–182), Cologne (69–72), Worms (437–440), Speyer (326–331), Trier (376–377), Prague (269–270), Bamberg (18), Regensburg (285–286); V. Colorni, *Legge ebraica e leggi locali*, Milan 1945, pp. 27–30; 34–43; B. Blumenkranz, 'Germany, 843–1096' [Hebrew] in: *The Dark Ages*, ed. C. Roth, Tel Aviv 1966, pp. 62–74; M. Toch, *Die Juden im mittelalterlichen Reich*, Munich 1998, pp. 5–7; E. Voltmer, 'Die Juden in den mittelalterlichen Städten des Rheingebiets,' in: *Juden in der Stadt*, eds. F. Mayrhofer and F. Opll, Linz 1999, pp. 119–143. The identification between Jews and Jewish involvement in trade was well known and familiar to all. See Aronius, *Regesten*, p. 29, No. 79 in the year 820, 'Per mansions omnium negotiatorum, sive in mercato sive aliubi negotientur, tam christianorum quam et Judaeorum'; by the end of the tenth century and the beginning of the eleventh, pp. 56, 59, Nos. 132, 140, 'Judeis et mercatoribus.'

17 R. Bonfil, 'The Cultural and Religious traditions of French Jewry in the Ninth Century, as Reflected in the Writings of Agobard of Lyons,' in: *Studies in Jewish Mysticism Philosophy and Ethical Literature*, eds. J. Dan and J. Haker [Hebrew], Jerusalem 1986, pp. 327–348, esp. p. 328, note 2, and Heil, 'Agobard, Amolo, das Kirchengut und die Juden von Lyon,' pp. 39–76; C. Merchavia, *The Church versus Talmudic and Midrashic Literature (500–1248)* [Hebrew], Jerusalem 1970, pp. 71–92. Bodo, bishop and chaplain of Emperor Louis the Pious: after a dissolute life at court, he made (838) a pilgrimage to Rome, was converted to Judaism, assuming the name of Eleazar, and married a Jewess.

18 N. Golb, 'Notes on the Conversion of European Christians to Judaism in the Eleventh Century,' *Journal of Jewish Studies* 16 (1965), pp. 69–74.

19 Browe, *Die Judenmission*, pp. 13, 184; B. Blumenkranz, *Juifs et Chretiens dans le monde accidental 430–1096*, Paris 1960, pp. 186, 139–144, 204–206, 232. J. Elukin, *Living Together, Living Apart*, Princeton 2007, pp. 17–60.

20 A. Grossman, *The Early Sages of Ashkenaz* [Hebrew], Jerusalem 1981, pp. 86–102; L. Raspe, 'Payyetanim as Heroes of Medieval Folk Narrative: The Case of R. Shimon B. Yishaq of Mainz,' in: the Schaefer Festschrift, *Jewish Studies between the Disciplines / Judaistik zwischen den Disziplinen: Papers in Honor of Peter Schäfer on the Occasion of his Sixtieth Birthday*, eds. K. Herrmann,

M. Schlüter, and G. Veltri, Leiden 2003, pp. 354–369. See also a more elaborate treatment in Raspe's book, *Jüdische Hagiographie im mittelalterlichen Aschkenas*, Tübingen 2006, ch. 5, pp. 242–322.

21 Rabbenu Gershom's liturgical writings were first used to derive historical conclusions by Katz, *Exclusiveness and Tolerance*, pp. 33–34, and this enterprise was expanded by Grossman in *The Early Sages of Ashkenaz*, pp. 162–165. See Gershom ben Judah [Meor ha-Golah], *Selihoth u-Phizmonum*, ed. A. Habermann, Jerusalem 1944, pp. 12, 19, 22, 33. *Piyyut* (pl. *Piyyutim*) is a lyrical composition intended to embellish an obligatory prayer or any other religious ceremony, communal or private.

22 A general term referring to a variety of prayer passages, primarily *piyyutim* characterized by expressions of regret for sins, mourning for the destruction of the Temple, and requests for God's forgiveness and for redemption.

23 Gershom ben Judah, *Selihoth u-Phizmonum*, pp. 8, 12–13.

24 Gershom ben Judah, *Selihoth u-Phizmonum*, *Eilekha niqra* ('We call to You'), pp. 12–13.

25 Gershom ben Judah, *Selihoth u-Phizmonum*, p. 13.

26 Gershom ben Judah, *Selihoth u-Phizmonum*, p. 13.

27 Grossman, *The Early Sages of Ashkenaz*, p. 12, notes 45–47.

28 The sages of the eleventh century reiterated his words; see Grossman, *The Early Sages of Ashkenaz*, p. 126.

29 The *kohen* is called up first in the synagogue to the ritual reading of the Torah, and he also blesses all the people during the course of the prayer service on festival days, reciting verses from Numbers 6:24–26 in a highly impressive ceremony in which he stands facing the congregation, raising his hands in blessing.

30 Based upon Leviticus 25:17: 'You shall not oppress each man his fellow'— interpreted in *b. Bava Metzi'a* 58b to refer to 'oppression through words.'

31 *Aliyah*—the rite of a member of a Jewish congregation being called to read from the Torah during religious services.

32 Gershom ben Judah, *Teshuvot Rabbenu Gershom Me'or haGola*, ed. S. Eidelberg, New York 1956, Nos. 4, 5; *Mahzor Vitry*, ed. S. Horowitz, Nuremberg 1892, No. 125; Isaac ben Moses, *Sefer Or Zarua*, 4 vols. Zhitomir 1862, Vol. 2, No. 412. See also *Tosafot Sotah* 39a s.v. *vekhi mehadar*; Katz, *Exclusiveness and Tolerance*, pp. 69–70; Grossman, *The Early Sages of Ashkenaz*, pp. 122–127; Perry, *Tradition and Transformation*, pp. 115–194.

33 Shlomo ben Isaac (Rashi), *Responsa Rashi*, ed. I. Elfenbein, New York 1943, No. 70, p. 82.

34 His responsum opens with the words: 'Thus was I shown from Heaven, that the apostate does not inherit,' despite the fact that he could have found a responsum in the literature of the Babylonian Geonim which he could have used in support of the same conclusion. Gershom ben Judah, *Teshuvot Rabbenu Gershom Me'or haGola*, No. 58, pp. 134–135.

35 *Teshuvot Rabbenu Gershom Me'or haGola*, No. 58, pp. 134–135; Meir ben Baruch, *Sheelot u-Teshuvot ha-Maharam*, Prague edition, ed. M. A. Blakh, Budapest 1895, No. 928. At the end of the thirteenth century, R. Asher ben Yehiel explained Rabbenu Gershom's words as follows: 'As he understood it, the intention was not that the convert to Christianity literally ceased to be his father's son and was cut off from Jewry, because we continue to see him as a Jew who has sinned; rather, because he has converted to Christianity, we penalize him by causing his inheritance to skip a generation, so that his relatives or sons and daughters who have remained Jews receive it instead of him.' See Asher ben Yehiel, *Shut haRosh*, ed. S. Yudelov, Jerusalem 1994, No. 17 §10.

36 Rashi recognizes that there would certainly be some among the Jewish community influenced by the degraded status of Jews in the Christian world whose 'hearts would stray' to Christianity and convert; these he termed idolatry worshippers. See Rashi to *b. Avodah Zarah* 54a s.v. *Vadai.*

37 In the book of Genesis, Joseph obeys the instruction of his father Jacob to seek his brothers who were minding the sheep near Shechem. Upon arriving there he does not find them, but instead encounters a man who, upon being asked where they are, answers, 'They have gone away from here.' Rashi Genesis 37:17 explains, 'They have gone away from brotherliness,' thereby anticipating the next stage in which the brothers attempt to kill Joseph or to sell him into slavery. The sin of the brothers, according to Rashi, lay in the fact that they did not relate to Joseph as a brother.

38 Katz, 'Even Though a Sinner,' pp. 203–227; Katz, *Exclusiveness and Tolerance*, pp. 67–81; A. Grossman, *The Early Sages of France* [Hebrew], Jerusalem 1995, pp. 154–155; Blidstein, 'Who is not a Jew,' pp. 369–390; Goldin, 'Juifs et juifs convertis au Moyen Age,' pp. 851–874.

39 Shlomo ben Isaac (Rashi), *Responsa Rashi*, No. 171.

40 *Halitzah*—the ritual releasing her from the need for levirate marriage.

41 Shlomo ben Isaac (Rashi), *Responsa Rashi*, No. 173.

42 Shlomo ben Isaac (Rashi), *Responsa Rashi*, No. 175.

43 Shlomo ben Isaac (Rashi), *Responsa Rashi*, No. 174.

44 A. Linder, *Roman Imperial Legislation on the Jews* [Hebrew], Jerusalem 1983, pp. 328–231, No. 52; Simonsohn, *The Apostolic See and the Jews*, pp. 202–203.

45 A. Agus, ed., *Responsa of the Tosaphists*, New York 1954, No. 9; Shlomo ben Isaac (Rashi), *Responsa Rashi*, Nos. 170, 171.

46 *b. Hullin* 5a; *Sanhedrin* 27a.

47 Shlomo ben Isaac (Rashi), *Responsa Rashi*, Nos. 170, 173, and 168 (regarding Responsum No. 168, it would seem that this was a responsum of Rabbenu Yitzhak, R'I, whose attribution to Rashi is questionable).

2

Forced conversion
during the First Crusade

The tendency that emerges from Rashi's words reflects a decisive leadership approach, establishing a clear direction of attempting to return converts to Christianity to Judaism. The self-definition of Judaism its leaders sought to establish was that of a religion that felt confident in its ability to deal with Christian theological claims and in its political ability to deal with the threat of forced conversion.

This situation changed during the course of the twelfth century and became far more complex, requiring a different sort of arrangement. During the course of the First Crusade (1096), the Jewish communities that were under the protection both of the emperor and of the bishops, who served as his representatives at the head of cities, were subjected to murderous attacks. The Christians violently forced Jews away from their religion and compelled them to become Christians; those who refused were either murdered or killed themselves as martyrs.[1] One of the leaders of the Jews called upon the emperor to protect them from the Christians who were setting out to liberate the Holy Sepulcher, and Henry IV responded to their pleas. When the emperor realized that his own warnings had come tragically late, he allowed those who had been forcibly converted to return to Judaism, notwithstanding the protests of Pope Clement III in his letter to the bishop of Bamberg.[2] On the face of it, the status of the Jews remained as it had been, and they continued to be a strong and self-confident group, enjoying the protection of the rulers. But in practice these attacks created a new reality, both in the eyes of the Christian population and for the Jews of France and Germany. Despite the fact that the actual extent of the attacks upon Jews at the end of the eleventh century was limited (only a few cities were affected: Worms, Mainz, Metz, Cologne, Regensburg, Prague, and perhaps Rouen), these events precipitated a psychological change throughout the region. Evidence of this may be found in Jewish writing from the twelfth century, even in those areas where very few Jews were attacked, or none at all.[3] This new situation found expression in two decisive directions for the Jewish community and its perception of substantive deviation—i.e., conversion to the rival religion. The first pertained to the manner in which Jews dealt with the campaign of forced conversion to Christianity during the Crusades in a number of cities of Germany. The second relates to the Jewish response to the success of the Christian conquest and the establishment of a Christian kingdom in the Holy Land.

At the end of the eleventh century, Christians set forth from Europe on a crusade to free the Holy Land, violently attempting to convert to Christianity the Jews they met on their way. While the harm to Jews was limited to certain cities in Germany, the impression left by this blow went far beyond the actual dimensions of the attacks. It became clear that the Christians were prepared to engage in violent behavior, whose purpose was to force conversion to Christianity—and this in cities where Jewish existence had seemed secure under the protection of the rulers. The Jewish response was to oppose the attempts at forced conversion, to the point of death. This martyr-like response to Christian violence became the preferred mode of Jewish behavior, thereby serving as one of the characteristics of Jewish self-definition. Moreover, in many cases, Jews anticipated the onslaught by Christians and killed themselves before the latter succeeded in forcibly converting them or in killing them. In this way, a considerable number of Jews killed themselves and even their families and children.

The generation that survived the First Crusade, and which educated its children in light of the Jewish response of 1096, left behind a limited number of sources, in prose and *piyyut* (religious poetry), revealing their attitude to the subject of forced conversion.[4] The authors of these sources describe the Gentiles—the burghers and the Crusaders—at great length, stressing that the goal of the Christians was first and foremost to convert the Jews to Christianity. Indeed, it was the Jews' description of the Crusaders' unrelenting cruelty towards them, the role played by the burghers, their former neighbors, and the bishops, who in their capacity as protectors of the city were supposed to defend them, that highlighted the missionary aim of Christian behavior which the Jewish texts sought to convey: the Christians were doing everything in their power to bring about the conversion of the Jews, and this was part of the new order in Europe which was the outcome of the Crusade itself. The Jewish texts emphasize this message whenever they write about the Christian perspective. Thus, for example, 'or let them

adopt our faith and acknowledge its [Judaism's] bastard offspring.' The
chroniclers describe incidents in which the Crusaders used the method of
'convert or we cut your throat here and now,' whereas the bishops adopted
a more indirect approach.[5] They did so not just to document the events
but, more important, to convince the twelfth-century readers that they
ought not to be deceived by 'proper' behavior and offers of protection, as
the Christians all had but one goal in mind—namely, to convert the Jews
to Christianity.

Twelfth-century liturgical poets likewise placed great emphasis on this
Christian goal. Two such writers portray Christian behavior as a trap that
had been set in order to ensnare the Jews. In his *piyyut*, Rabbi Eliezer ben
Nathan of Mainz (1090–1170) warns that the Christians are laying a trap
for the Jews, and that after they are extricated they will be killed.[6] Rabbi
Kalonymus ben Yehudah writes that the Christians are attempting to
convince the Jews to convert to Christianity by using words: 'They start a
debate with you and argue … Their words and promises are snares.' This
piyyut emphatically argues that the Christians aspire primarily to convert
and not to kill.[7]

Jewish writings describing what happened in Germany when the
Crusaders attacked the Jews in the Christian cities have been the subject
of extensive research. These writings are the product of members of the
first generation following the Crusades, who gathered and documented
sources and letters from the First Crusade, constructing an 'educational
narrative' of great significance, essentially a code of behavior that was
completed even before the Second Crusade.[8] This generation shaped the
consciousness of those Jews who came after the First Crusade, for whom
the idea of martyrdom served as a cornerstone of proper Jewish behavior.
In this way, they preserved the self-image of their own generation and that
of its parent's generation, not only as willing to die in order to prove the
truth of the Jewish religion and its victory but also as those who in fact
realized this willingness and died as martyrs, and even killed others in
order to prevent their 'falling' into the hands of Christians and Christianity.
The examples they used needed to be reliable, for they were addressing a
public which had itself experienced these events or heard of them from
those who had experienced first hand what happened during the course of
the First Crusade. Hence, the authors of these chronicles do not conceal
the fact that quite a number of Jews had submitted to the forced attempts
by the Christians to convert them to Christianity, as they were acting at
a time when records and memories of these events were still fresh and
familiar. Part of their audience may have itself been forced to convert

against its will. It was in relation to this that they were able to shape their message and to define their own identity. The message which emerges from the chronicles is that most of the Jews chose to die a martyr's death, and only a small minority preferred to convert to Christianity—and that only in appearance.

There is a great deal of emphasis on the fact that the converts to Christianity were small in number, and that even these did so under coercion, acting unwillingly, when they were surprised, confused, and so forth. They are described with the help of a series of diminutive terms, such as 'very few' or 'a few grains.' The most striking examples occurred in Regensburg and Metz, where there was in actuality massive conversion. According to the chronicles, they were forced down to the river, and they made 'a bad sign over the river.' One should not speak contemptuously of these forced converts: they attempted to return to Judaism, and even when in Christian captivity attempted to observe Judaism as far as possible.[9] Even this small minority of 'forced apostates' underwent a shocking and terrible experience when they were converted; hence the only conclusion to be reached was that it was better to die a martyr's death than to live as a Christian. In the final analysis, the fashioning of the self- and future-image of the Jews in the twelfth century was of the Jew who was unwilling to become a Christian, even if forced to do so.

There were, however, those who nevertheless did convert. According to the chronicles, all those people who changed their religion did so out of noble reasons; all of them discovered the poverty entailed in their deviation as opposed to the power of the accepted norm; all of them plan for themselves a death that will emphasize the norm, even more so those who kill themselves for the norm. The most striking example of this in the texts is the conversion and death of R. Yitzhak ben David ha-Parnas[10] who initially agreed to convert to Christianity because he was caught within a net of circumstances that (seemingly) did not allow any other option: he was concerned about his property, he was worried about his sick and elderly mother, and it was clear to him that his children would be taken by the Christians and raised as Christians. The rationale he offered himself was that, as a Christian, he would be able to safeguard his (Jewish) property, take care of his mother, and be close to his children and oversee their education. Nevertheless, at a certain moment, while he was alone in the synagogue opposite the Holy Ark, he understood that none of these reasons could compare to the commended form of Jewish behavior, which he summarizes in a sentence pregnant with significance: 'I will repent, and be innocent and whole before the Lord God of Israel, until I pay him with my soul and fall into His hands; perhaps He will act in accordance with His great mercy and I will join my friends, and together with them enter into their realm.' In brief: there are no good reasons for converting to Christianity. Purity is emphasized in contradistinction to becoming a Christian. The dead martyrs doubtless are proof of this, but even those who had, temporarily, joined the Christian religion will in the end understand this. His self-sacrifice, in the final event, will surely come about, fashioned as a sin-offering. This motif likewise emerges from the story of R. Yitzhak ha-Levi, a person who was forcibly converted to Christianity after being subjected to harsh beatings until 'he did not understand anything.' Once he realized what he had done, three days later, he returned to his home in Cologne, stayed there a little while, and then went to the Rhine and drowned himself in the river. He wished, by means of this water, to erase the impression of that water which had turned him into a Christian. His body floated along the Rhine until it arrived at the village of Neuss, where it was expelled onto the shore alongside that of R. Shmuel ben Asher, known as 'the *Hasid*' ('the pious one'), who had been killed at the riverbank together with his two sons. The story concludes, according to this version, with the words: 'And those two pious men were buried together in the sand on the banks of the river, in a single grave, and they sanctified the name of Heaven before the sun.' The person who had been converted to Christianity by force atoned for his act by a glorious death, and thereby unquestionably merited to be numbered among the martyrs.[11]

The message conveyed by the chronicles regarding those Jews who adopted Christianity during the first half of the twelfth century and, all the more so, of those who remained in the fold, is clearly seen in a section that was definitely written after the events (it is phrased in the past tense) by the editor or the interpreter of the testimonies and stories discussed above.[12] This section, generally considered a polemic against Christianity, is meant to encourage those Jews living in the difficult circumstances of the beginning of the twelfth century. I would like to call attention to the second half of this section, which should be read as a statement addressed to the Jews, a polemic against their brethren who converted to Christianity in the twelfth century:

> Then will they comprehend, understand, and take to heart that in folly they have cast our bodies to the ground, and for falsehood have they slain our saints; that they have spilled the blood of righteous women because of a putrid corpse, and shed the blood of sucklings over the teachings of an agitator and misleader; that his teachings are folly and that they do

not know their Creator, nor walk on a virtuous path or an upright way; that they were not wise and did not take to heart Who it is that made the ocean and the dry land; and that in all their actions they were fools and simpletons. Good sense abandoned them, and they placed their trust in folly, neither recognizing nor declaring the Name of the living God, King of the Universe, who is Eternal and everlasting. May the blood of His devoted ones stand us in good stead and serve as atonement for us and for our posterity after us, and for our children's children eternally, like the Binding of our father Isaac when our Father Abraham bound him upon the altar. These saints did not say to one another: 'Have mercy on yourselves,' but rather 'Let us cast our blood like water on the ground, and may it be considered before the Blessed Holy One as the blood of the gazelle and of the hart.' ... Thus have attested those few survivors who were forcibly converted. They heard with their own ears and saw with their own eyes the actions of these saints and their utterances at the time of their slaughter and murder.[13]

The aim of the Christian groups which attacked the Jews in the Rhine Valley, according to those sparse and contradictory sources written by the Christians themselves, is unclear. Had they decided to make all of Europe Christian by forcibly converting the Jews to Christianity, or did they wish to make Europe Christian by eliminating all the Jews?[14] The Jewish sources describing the First Crusade, in both prose and liturgical poetry, make it clear that, as they perceived it, the tendency of the Christians was new, revolutionary, and absolute. The Jews identified the various attitudes of the Christians to the state of Christianity in the world, from which they understood that the Christians were setting out on a crusade to bring about Christian rule over the world, and that the moment the grave of the Christian Messiah in Palestine was freed, it would be impossible, according to this new Christian perception, for there to remain any Jews in the world: either they would convert, or they must die!

This tendency is implied by three chronicles that describe what happened when the Crusader armies passed through the Rhine Valley during the First Crusade. One ought to focus here specifically upon the source written by Rabbi Eliezer ben Nathan (Ra'avan) because he describes the event as he experienced it as a six-year-old child, and what he concluded from it during his mature years (it seems reasonable to assume that he wrote it before the Second Crusade in 1146). He strongly emphasizes that the Christians were interested in converting the Jews and that only after they were convinced that the Jews were steadfast in their refusal to convert were they killed. In the eyes of Ra'avan, the options confronting the Christians were either 'we shall take revenge on them and make them cease to be a people' or 'they shall become like us.'[15] Ra'avan underlines this from the beginning of his prose account, in which he describes a Jewish woman who killed herself in Speyer, and goes on to admit the violent conversion of large groups of Jews (who did not kill themselves). Hence, the true intention of the 'Crusaders' is not important, because the Jews defined the Christian intention as imposing Christian religion on all of them, first and foremost on the Jewish children, and whoever would not agree to this would be killed.

The Crusader movement had explicitly folk-missionary characteristics. During the Second Crusade, Bernard of Clairvaux attempted to prevent violent behavior involving either forcible conversion or murder of the Jews, but he was unable to suppress the missionary motif, which had been previously planted in the Crusader propaganda.[16] Anyone reading the Christian chronicle, *The Annals of Würzburg*, alongside the writings of Rabbi Ephraim of Bonn, can see this. Rabbi Ephraim of Bonn describes incidents of forced conversion on different dates in the second half of the twelfth century in Germany. There are numerous examples to illustrate that the aim of the Christians was to forcibly impose the Christian religion upon the Jews, and that such conversion would save the Jews from death. According to Jewish sources, even those Jews who were suspected of murder or of blood libels could save themselves from punishment if they converted to Christianity. So long as the overt Christian behavior was such, it was possible to portray the turning of Jews to the Christian world as based essentially upon violent coercion, and thereby mitigate the negative attitude towards Jews who voluntarily converted to the rival religion.

From the beginning of the twelfth century onwards, the norm dictated by the educational process was one of opposition to forced conversion to Christianity to the point of death. In terms of the Jewish self-definition, one might still relate to Jews who had converted through having been forced to do so. But how could one continue relating to them as 'brothers who erred' when the norm required resistance to the point of death, and even putting oneself to death? From the moment that the Jewish self-definition included, in addition to the regular definitions, absolute unwillingness to convert to the rival religion, even by force (i.e., strict and extreme martyrdom behavior, in which the Jew had to be prepared, not only to die, but also to kill himself and his family), the attitude towards the convert to Christianity had to be defined anew, both from the popular viewpoint and from the halakhic perspective. As a result of the strong emphasis on this motif, it became clear that, even if the halakhic attitude towards apostates continued to see them in theory as 'brethren' who had been forcibly converted to the rival religion, the basic folk attitude towards them would be different; the very self-definition by the Jew as such made it difficult to continue to relate to them as 'brethren' for whom the door of repentance was always open.

Notes

1 R. Chazan, *European Jewry and the First Crusade*, Berkeley 1987; R. Chazan, *God, Humanity, and History: The Hebrew First Crusade Narratives*, Berkeley 2000; S. Goldin, *The Ways of Jewish Martyrdom*, Turnhout 2008.

2 A. Habermann, ed., *Sefer Gezerot Ashkenaz ve-Zarfat*, Jerusalem 1945, p. 94; J. Aronius, *Regesten zur Geschichte der Juden im fränkischen und deutschen Reiche bis zum Jahre 1273*, Berlin 1902, Nos. 203, 204; J. Elukin, 'The Discovery of the Self: Jews and Conversion in the Twelfth Century,' in: *Jews and Christians in Twelfth-Century Europe*, eds. M. Signer and J. Van Engen, Notre Dame, Ind. 2001, pp. 63–76.

3 J. W. Parkes, *The Conflict of the Church and the Synagogue*, London 1934, pp. 79–81; J. Elukin, 'From Jew to Christian? Conversion and Immutability in Medieval Europe,' in: *Varieties of Religious Conversion in the Middle Ages*, ed. J. Muldoon, Gainesville, Fla. 1997, pp. 171–189.

4 A. S. Abulafia, 'The Interrelationship between the Hebrew Chronicles of the First Crusade,' *Journal of Semitic Studies* 27 (1982), pp. 221, 239, Nos. 8–15, 61–65; Chazan, *European Jewry*, pp. 40–49, 307–308, Nos. 7–22. I. G. Marcus, 'Review of Robert Chazan, "European Jewry and the First Crusade,"' *Speculum* 64 (1989), pp. 685–688; I. G. Marcus, 'History, Story and Collective Memory: Narrativity in Early Ashkenazic Culture,' *Prooftexts* 10 (1990), pp. 365–388; R. Chazan, 'Factivity of Medieval Narrative: A Case Study of the Hebrew First Crusade Narrative,' *Association for Jewish Studies Review* 16 (1991), pp. 31–56; Goldin, *The Ways of Jewish Martyrdom*, pp. 85–162; E. Haverkamp, *Hebraische Berichte uber die Judenverfolgungen wahrend des ersten Kreuzzugs, Monumenta Germaniae historica. Hebraische Texte aus dem mittelalterlichen Deutschland*, Hannover 2005.

5 Habermann, *Sefer Gezerot Ashkenaz ve-Zarfat*, pp. 24, 27, 29, 41, 44, 46, 63, 97. English translation, S. Eidelberg, *The Jews and the Crusaders*, Madison 1977.

6 Habermann, *Sefer Gezerot Ashkenaz ve-Zarfat*, p. 85.

7 Habermann, *Sefer Gezerot Ashkenaz ve-Zarfat*, pp. 64–66. The imagery is taken from Jeremiah 5:26, according to the King James version: 'For among my people are found wicked men: they lay wait, as he that setteth snares; they set a trap, they catch men.' It is worthwhile to note Rashi's explanation of this verse: 'When the trap that the hunter sets to snare foxes in the woods wounds the leg which is caught inside, it clamps down and seizes his leg and he is trapped; it is [apparently] called "piege," which comes from "pied" [in French].'

8 S. Goldin, 'The Socialisation for "Kidush ha-Shem" among Medieval Jews,' *Journal of Medieval History* 23 (1997), pp. 117–138.

9 Habermann, *Sefer Gezerot Ashkenaz ve-Zarfat*, pp. 23, 67–68, 81, 103.

10 This is an example with which two of my colleagues, Israel Yuval and Jeremy Cohen, have dealt. Yuval attributed to the process of this man's death a model of a ceremony of offering a sacrifice, whose purpose was to bring about the 'vengeful redemption'—I. J. Yuval, *Two Nations in Your Womb*, Berkeley 2006, pp. 144–154; J. Cohen, *Sanctifying the Name of God*, Philadelphia 2004, pp. 91–101; J. Cohen, 'Between Martyrdom and Apostasy: Doubt and Self-Definition in the Twelfth-Century Ashkenaz,' *Journal of Medieval and Early Modern Studies* 29 (1999), pp. 431–471.

11 Habermann, *Sefer Gezerot Ashkenaz ve-Zarfat*, pp. 44, 78.

12 Habermann, *Sefer Gezerot Ashkenaz ve-Zarfat*, p. 43.

13 Regarding the Christians and the Jewish behavior, see: Habermann, *Sefer Gezerot Ashkenaz ve-Zarfat*, pp. 26–27, see Eidelberg translation *The Jews and the Crusaders*, pp. 25–26: 'You are the children of those who killed our object of veneration. We are his children and it is therefore obligatory for us to avenge him. Your God has never been at peace with you.' The Jewish reaction: 'When we heard these words, our hearts trembled and moved out of their places. We were dumb with silence, abiding in darkness, like those long dead, waiting for the Lord to look forth and behold from heaven.'

14 K. Stow, 'Conversion, Apostasy, and Apprehensiveness: Emicho of Flonheim and the Fear of Jews in the Twelfth Century,' *Speculum* 76 (2001), pp. 911–933; D. Malkiel, 'Destruction or Conversion: Intention and Reaction, Crusaders and Jews, in 1096,' *Jewish History* 15 (2001), pp. 257–280.

15 Habermann, *Sefer Gezerot Ashkenaz ve-Zarfat*, p. 72.

16 A. Haverkamp, 'Baptised Jews in German Lands during the Twelfth Century,' in: *Jews and Christians in Twelfth Century Europe*, eds. M. A. Signer and J. Van Engen, Notre Dame, Ind., pp. 261–262, esp. notes 36–42.

3

Theological confrontation with Christianity's success

The success of the Christians in defeating the Muslims in the Holy Land, conquering it and establishing a Christian colony there, particularly in the Holy City of Jerusalem, was a harsh blow to the Jews from a theological viewpoint. The theological difficulty, which emerged during the course of the twelfth century, became a central issue, one which also affected the status of voluntary converts to Christianity. The Jewish sources are ominously silent concerning the conquest of the Holy Land by Christians and the establishment of a Christian city in Jerusalem. From the viewpoint of twelfth-century Jewry, there was no point in publicizing this fact, which reinforced the powerful Christian theological claim that their victories and worldly success were proof that God had abandoned the Jewish people and now supported the Christian side. In reading Jewish sources from the twelfth century, one is hard put to find even an echo of the historical events which occurred in the Land of Israel. The chronicles describing the First Crusade relate to events in Europe alone, leaving the reader with the impression that the Crusaders moved eastward, where they were stopped and slaughtered by their Christian brethren. There is no reference to the fact that in July 1099 Jerusalem was conquered decisively by the Christians. Anyone reading the Jewish chronicles of the Second Crusade gains the impression they speak of European matters and of movements within that continent. Only after Saladin defeated the Christians at the Battle of the Horns of Hattin (Karnei-Hittin) in 1187 does the Jewish reader discover that there were Christians in Palestine and that they were defeated by the Muslims, who slaughtered them and stole their sacred objects.[1]

Nevertheless, one may find an echo of the Jewish theological frustration in light of the political situation and the Christian victories. In only one source, that of R. Yitzhak ben Saadya, does the author of the *piyyut* depict this problem in a heartfelt manner, without any attempt at concealment. The *piyyut*, *Eikh ukhal lavo eilekha* ('How can I come before You'), has survived in the collection of *Selihot* recited by Ashkenazic Jews during the Ten Days of Penitence between Rosh Hashanah and Yom Kippur.[2] In this *piyyut*, as in most liturgical poems of this genre, the Jewish believer bewails the situation of Exile, of the Jews being miserable and downtrodden, dwelling among the Gentiles, yet longing for closeness to God. In addition, the author emphasizes the theological tension between his Judaism and the success of the surrounding Christianity, particularly that related to the conquest of the Land of Israel by the Christians. In my opinion, this *piyyut* was written in Europe during the course of the twelfth century, as the Christians are described there a proud nation, its people considering themselves wise men, dwelling in security, joy, and comfort, and mocking the Jews. Here, for the first time, there is also an allusion to the Christian conquest of the Holy Land.

The Christians are referred to in this *piyyut* as *ovdei zulatekha* ('those who serve [a divinity] other than You'—i.e., those generally referred to as idolaters). This is a striking expression, which immediately guides the reader towards the central-most place in the prayer: 'O Lord, there is none like You, and there is no God other than You' [זולתך] (a quotation from 1 Chronicles 17:20). This verse is associated with a midrash which draws a connection between the word 'other than You' and the compulsion to worship idols.[3] The midrash links this verse in turn to Isaiah 26:13, 'O Lord our God, we have been swallowed by masters other than You,' seeking a connection between these two verses in which the word *zulatekha*, 'apart from You,' appears. The midrash's answer is: 'They demanded of us to serve their idolatry, like a husband who demands intercourse of his wife.' The Christians, says the *paytan*, not only prevent the Jews from observing their religion, but seek to remove them from it, and thereby separate them from their God.[4]

According to the author, the Christian theological claim is that at this point they are wearing 'My garment'—i.e., the glorious garment of the people of Israel—and are eating 'milk and honey' (an expression mentioned twenty-six times in the Bible in connection with the Land of Israel), being chosen by God. Our author describes a situation in which the Jews are surrounded by both Muslims and Christians, and he explicitly mentions the Christian claim that the verse, 'The greater shall serve the younger' (Genesis 25:23) is part of the punishment of the Jews. The Christians refer to 'a man who has never prophesied' as a prophet, but in his name they make a great and mighty army, proud of its military ability; they have kings and dominions and are victorious everywhere. Their situation proves the Christians' claim that the Jews are weak, dispersed, without rule or 'government,' subject to the hands of Gentiles who do not understand their language. Our poetic author knows that their truth is derived not only from the successful place of the Christians in the world, but also from the fact that the circumstances of Judaism and Jews are similar to those described in the prophecies of wrath in the Torah. At the climax of the poem, the author describes the unbelievable situation ('Who would believe?') according to which 'those who hate purity'—i.e., the Christians—dwell in the Land of Israel, are wealthy and secure, and occupy the Temple site ('dwell in My Sanctuary').

The *piyyut* is composed of eleven stanzas, each one of which consists of three lines describing the success of the Christians, while the fourth emphasizes the miserable situation of the Jews. The Christians are powerful, victorious, wise, knowledgeable, enjoy rule and government, are wealthy, and dwell (he uses the verb *shokhen*, associated with the Temple!) in the palace of the Jew (i.e., Jerusalem). On the other hand, while the Jew has not abandoned his God, neither is he close to God ('I have not been called to go to the king'). He is like a docile lamb, ignorant and without knowledge, within the Exile, childless and bereft, shamed, impoverished, and beaten. The author concludes with a prayer for the future coming of the House of the Lord.[5]

Even if we assume that this literary example is not complete, it is impossible to ignore that, from the middle of the twelfth century on, Jewish leadership anticipated a concrete danger of Jewish conversion to Christianity arising, not from the violent struggle of the Christians against Judaism but rather from their ability to persuade and to convince. The success of Christianity led to the phenomenon of Jews who converted to Christianity of their own free will, of a type whom the Jews could no longer label as 'forced converts.' During the course of the twelfth century we find evidence of such converts to Christianity in the Jewish sources.

One such example appears in an inquiry addressed to Rabbi Ya'akov ben Meir, Rabbenu Tam (ca. 1100–71, Ramerupt, northern France), asking whether the *get* (divorce writ) of a convert should bear his Jewish name only, or his new Christian name as well. This was obviously a family in which the husband alone had decided to convert, while his wife remained Jewish. Rabbenu Tam's response draws attention to the fact that conversion to Christianity had become a part of Jewish life. He writes that 'more than twenty writs of divorce (*gittin*) of converts were made in Paris and France.' In order to provide the questioner with an example related to his conclusion regarding the names of the converts, R. Tam notes, as if in passing, the names of two apostates hailing from different towns: 'Did you ever hear of a convert named Asher of Cologne or Avran of Sens?' His answer implies that these were converts from prominent families, that he knew of cases from Germany as well, and that the general public related to these converts to Christianity by labeling them with derogatory names or nicknames in order to avoid calling them by their new Christian names. And, although twenty divorce writs for converts is a very substantial number, this tells us nothing about the totality of converts, but only of those who agreed to give a *get* to their wives who had remained within the fold of Judaism. Indeed, there were also converts who refused to grant their wives a *get*, and still other cases in which the entire family converted. In any event, in small communities such as those discussed here, twenty bills of divorce is an extremely significant number, attesting to an extensive, although not mass, phenomenon.[6]

Such conversion to Christianity was a new phenomenon. Jews rushed to convert to Christianity, were convinced of its truth, and were also interested in convincing their former brethren (i.e., the Jews) of the truth of Christianity. Fortunately, we have the testimony of a Jew who converted to Christianity during this specific time period. Yehuda-Herman was a Jew born in the city of Cologne in 1107, about one decade after the destruction of its Jewish community during the First Crusade; he was baptized as a Christian in Cologne in 1128, and became a monk in the Kapenberg monastery. In 1148, twenty years after his conversion, he wrote his autobiography. This work has been extensively studied, both because of its rarity as the confession of a Jew who converted and explained his motives, and because it is among the earliest examples of the autobiographical genre. Our interest in it in the context of the present study is not related to either of these two aspects but rather to the question of the attitude of the Jewish group towards the apostate and the reasons he cites for his conversion. In 1988, Avraham Saltman raised the possibility that this work was an educational fiction—that is, a work written by monks in order to convince the reader of the truth of Christianity. Most scholars do not accept this theory, and I likewise tend to believe that the contents of this work are authentic in substance, although one cannot completely ignore the points raised by Saltman regarding the educational aim of the work.[7]

For our purposes, there are a number of important points emphasized by Yehuda-Herman in his story. One is that his basic sense of repugnance towards his brethren, his family, and his Jewish relatives derived from the Jews' love of profit and their lust for money and property. Secondly, it is clear from his story that from the moment his relatives identified his tendency towards Christianity, they kept their eyes on him to prevent him drawing closer. However, it would seem that the youth's anger and his own personal fears affected his mature writing so that those sections seem particularly vivid, but it does seem reasonable to assume that those in his immediate Jewish environment kept an eye on him from the moment they began to suspect his religious deviation.

According to his account, at age thirteen he had a dream filled with awesome grandeur and extremely significant, to which he attributes the beginning of his transition to Christianity. He saw a king approaching him and giving him an impressive white horse, an elaborate belt, a bag of silk, and heavy gold coins. The king preferred him above all the members of his own nobility, rode in his company, and even ate with him from the same plate. This dream made a deep impression upon him, but when he told it to one of his relatives, who was 'a man of authority among the Jews,' the latter interpreted it as signs of material success—a beautiful woman who would be his wife, great wealth, and worldly honor. In the story, Herman emphasizes that the interpretation of the dream by the Jew was consistent with the Jewish characteristic (Romans 8:5) of interpreting everything in terms of the pursuit of wealth. As a Christian, he was convinced that the correct interpretation of the dream was the appearance of Divine grace, which was given him by the 'Christian' God. In order to prove this, he tells of his trip at age twenty to Mainz for purposes of trade, and his encounter there with the prince-bishop of Münster, Egbert. He was so impressed by the bishop's personality that he gave him a loan without taking any collateral. When this became known to the Jews, they cursed and reviled him, as he ought to have taken a collateral twice the size of the loan; the Jews forced him to return to the bishop in order to get either the money or the pledge, as required. The mature author states here that 'the Jews are all completely enslaved to business.' The Christians whom he meets along his path are utterly different. The bishop's helper, a man named Rikmar, foregoes the gifts he has received and gives them to him. Moreover, Yehuda-Herman, the classical Christianizer, emphasizes that he was also impressed by the miracles that enabled him to decide on his path, but that the Christian bishop was interested that a Jew would convert to Christianity because he was convinced of the truth of Christianity, out of faith and not due to the influence of a miracle.

The second point is emphasized in his description of the contrast between the pressured, frightening, and vulgar Jewish atmosphere and the calm, innocent and accepting atmosphere among the Christians. The Jews are afraid to let him be free, and hire an elderly man to accompany him wherever he goes on his trip to the bishop, to keep an eye on him, and to report back to his family about his actions. And indeed, that is what the person did. When Herman returned to Cologne and the bishop of course paid his debt, the suspicions of the 'carnal' Jews were disproven. His escort, who had accused him of becoming friendly with Christians and listening to them, is promptly punished by God with a vengeance, becoming ill and suffering a terribly painful death. The Jews continue to follow him, and connect him with their own destiny by forcing him to marry a young girl whom he had betrothed. When they see that he refrains from coming to the synagogue, they attempt to kill him, sending letters denigrating him to Mainz, where he is to flee in the future. In his book, the apostate Yehuda-Herman not only confirms that there were apostate Jews who converted to Christianity of their own free will, but describes in a striking way the atmosphere of tension and suspicion that existed in the Jewish community regarding this phenomenon.

The tendency towards fascination with Christianity likewise emerges from a Jewish source from the end of the twelfth century in England, which speaks of the suicide of a 'venerable and very wealthy Talmud scholar who studied in the yeshiva, R. Yom Tov,' who killed himself on the eve of Shavuot. We are told by this source that this Yom Tov was harassed by a demon who showed him the form of 'warp and woof'—i.e., the cross—and tried to persuade him to engage in idolatry. The source adds that Yom Tov's father, upon hearing of this, did not leave his room, did not interrupt his studies, and did not shed a single tear. The father's behavior may have been because of the son's suicide, which is prohibited according to halakhah or, what seems more likely, as an expression of the problematic nature of this son, who was evidently 'fascinated' by Christianity and drew close to it, a phenomenon described by the author in terms of a demon attacking the young son.[8]

Many scholars have noted that the Jews of the Middle Ages lived among Christians and were familiar with the Christian religion, and that it fascinated and tempted them. The struggle against the attraction of Christianity, with which the Jews had to contend, was the outcome of fear and the desire to integrate into society and succeed economically, as well as theological persuasion. Several scholars have dealt with this issue and invoked various proofs in support of their views. Here I wish to deal with an interesting source which, I believe, can illustrate this phenomenon very well. I refer to a commentary by Rabbi Abraham ben R. Azriel (thirteenth century) on a *piyyut* by R. Solomon ben Judah ha-Bavli, which appears in R. Abraham's book, *Arugat ha-Bosem*. Rabbi Solomon ha-Bavli (mid-tenth century) evidently lived in northern Italy, although his family was of Oriental origin. When R. Abraham saw this *piyyut* it was already accompanied by commentary, but he added another level of interpretation. In other words, we have here at least three layers: the first, the *piyyut* of R. Solomon ha-Bavli; the second, the commentary ascribed to R. Joseph Kara that preceded that of R. Abraham; and the third, Rabbi Abraham's thirteenth-century interpretation.

The *piyyut*, entitled *Ahashvah la-Da'at Amal* ('I shall consider [think about] knowing labor'), is of the *zulat* type which was recited by the leader and congregation on Shabbat Bereshit, the Sabbath on which the cycle of reading the Torah was renewed. The *piyyut* alludes to the human tendency to absorb the wonders of one's surroundings.

The first commentator phrased his interpretation of the word 'to absorb' in an amazing way: 'Even though my mind absorbs the magic of the Christian surroundings, and it penetrates my being as a flame and tempts me to follow it, my closeness to God comforts me and prevents me from succumbing to it.' This interpretation was obviously written before the thirteenth century. Rabbi Abraham's response was that there is nothing surprising about the words of the previous commentator because, in the end, he emphasizes that his closeness to God triumphs over any temptation or false magic. He cites Rashi's commentary on a verse in Psalm 73, stating that God confronts His people with difficult and terrible situations in order to reward them with the life of the World to Come. Moreover, he stresses that jealousy and temptation come from observing the serenity in which the Christians live. This interpretation again underscores just how tempting Christianity was and the extent to which the Jews had to contend with it and its temptations. Only the believer's closeness to God can save him from this temptation.

As Jordan notes in an important article, an interesting characteristic of these converts to Christianity is their age. We are dealing here with the conversion of educated young people from good families.[9] One cannot ignore the fact that, from the middle of the twelfth century on, the Jewish leadership anticipated a concrete danger of Jewish conversion that would stem not from the violent struggle of Christianity against Judaism, but rather from its ability to fascinate and to persuade.

Against this tendency, there developed among the Jews in the twelfth and thirteenth centuries a polemical literature intended for internal purposes, a special section of which is devoted to the matter of apostates. It was clear to the authors of this polemical literature that at that time there were apostate Jews among the Christians, and that it was they who taught the Christians the arguments of the Jews. The polemical books fulfill a three-fold function: to strengthen Jews against Christian arguments, to serve as propaganda against converts to Christianity, and to persuade apostates to return to Judaism.[10]

The author of *Sefer Yosef ha Mekane*, R. Joseph ben Nathan Official, who lived in twelfth-century France, describes the character of the 'theological' convert as perceived by the Jews. He wrote this book in reaction to the Christians (monks, priests, bishops, a pope, members of certain orders, and disreputable characters) and apostates who attempted to convince Jews to convert to Christianity. 'The transgressors, members of our nation, have abandoned the source of living waters [their faith], to pursue vacuity, to boast that they are the prophets of truth, to exalt the name of Jesus, to pay heed to falsehoods.' To R. Joseph it was clear that these apostates had been indoctrinated by Christianity. They were 'orthodox in their worship of idols' (*avodah zarah*), believing in the Christian 'truth' with all their heart, and hoping to convince the Jews of the truth of the 'dead one' (i.e., Jesus).

Among other things, these converts attempted to persuade the Jews of the doctrine of the Trinity and the truth of the 'New Testament,' and to convince them that the Virgin Mary was the mother of Jesus, that Jesus was the Messiah, that he had come, that God had turned away from the people of Israel, that they were no longer the chosen people, and even that the Christians were physically beautiful while the Jews were offensive. They argued about Rashi's commentaries, about the problem of evil in the world, about Mary's having corrected the wrong done by Eve, about the forbidden foods and, of course, they claimed enthusiastically that the Hebrew Bible, particularly the Song of Songs, contained hints of Jesus' coming, that the Torah has been abrogated by the coming of Jesus, and that God was no longer interested in the repentance of the Jews.[11]

Sefer Nizzahon Vetus, or the 'Old Book of Polemic,' is an anthology of attacks on Christian belief and its principles or, as its subtitle has it, 'A critique of the Gospels and Christianity.' The book is organized according to the order of chapters of the Hebrew Bible and includes most of the books of the Bible as well as extensive reference to the New Testament. It was written at the end of the thirteenth century, and based upon earlier collections which were written in Germany and in northern France.[12] But the role of the apostate is not the main focus of *Nizzahon Vetus* as it is in *Sefer Yosef ha Mekane*. Rather, the description of the convert serves here as an antithesis to the Jew who remains faithful to his God: "'And I will purge out from among you the rebels and transgressors" (Ezekiel 20:38)—these are the apostates who accept their defiling baptism, rebelling against God and denying him.' The apostate is described as an 'evil Jew' whose aim is to eat any food, to drink any wine, to whore and 'to relinquish the yoke of heaven, no longer to have any fear, to free himself from all commandments and to become contaminated with sins, and lapse, woe unto him, into the life of the moment; we should therefore, not be surprised by his evil deeds.' The convert is even accused, like the Christians and 'evil ones,' of preventing the end of the Exile and its sufferings.[13]

Nizzahon Vetus gives sharp expression to the aggression and feelings of disgust towards the convert to Christianity. The aggressiveness and extremism in the book relate to the apostates who have converted to Christianity and are now playing an active part in the polemic itself, where they represent Christian ideas and what they present as proofs for the correctness of Christianity and its theological superiority to Judaism.

The author cites those verses and subjects which are specifically brought by the apostate. For example, they attempt to prove the Christian truth by invoking the verse 'until Shiloh comes and to him' (Genesis 49:10), in which Shiloh represents Jesus.[14] Similarly, the very use in the Torah of the word *Elohim*, in the plural, is taken up to confirm the Christian claim that God is both father and son.[15] The author suggests to his Jewish readers a linguistic answer to this claim that puts to ridicule the Christians' distorted understanding, as it is well known that out of respect one habitually addresses kings and nobility using the plural form; all the more so God.

The author likewise cites the claim, or 'proof,' of the apostates that the phrase used by God, 'Let us make man' (Genesis 1:26) proves the doctrine of God as both father and son. Here he presents the decisive response given by Jews against those who convert to Christianity, an answer made up of two components: the one explaining the context and the other ridiculing the Christian approach which the converts had taken upon themselves. On the first level, the author explains that God's words, 'Let us make' are addressed to the spirit that God breathes into the soil/dust which comes from the earth.[16] On the second level, he composes a mocking and satirical story containing an ironic dialogue between the 'Father'—i.e., God—and His 'son,' Jesus:

> Indeed, the matter is as you say. The father told the son 'My son, help me, and let you and I make a man.' However, the son rebelled and did not wish to help his father, and so the father made man alone without the son's help, as it is written 'and God created man,' with a singular rather than a plural verb. Consequently, the father became angry with his son and said, 'If the

time should come when you need my assistance, I shall not help you just
as you have not helped me.' So when the day came for the son to be stoned
and hanged, he cried out in a bitter voice 'My Lord, my Lord, why have
you forsaken me? Why are you so far from saving me ... ?' and he begged
for his help [Matt. 27:46]. Then the father told him, 'When I asked you to
help me make man, you rebelled against me and did not come to the aid of
the Lord, and so my own power availed me and I made him without you.
Now you too help yourself, for I shall not come to your aid.'[17]

Beyond the level of theological debate with those who had been
convinced by Christianity, there clearly emerges here the anger against
converts to Christianity who made use of knowledge they had acquired
when they were Jews, from Jewish sources and especially from the Talmud,
in order to attack the arguments of the Jews in a fallacious manner, thereby
proving their mistaken approach. The anger and sense of disgust relate to
this double betrayal. For example, in Genesis 47:31 it is told that the dying
Jacob bowed down upon his bed. The apostate, referring to the word
'bed,' *mitah*, which is written without the letter *yod*, and thus may be read
as identical to *mateh*, 'staff,' inferred that the dying Jacob bowed down
to the cross resting at the head of his bed. He exploits his knowledge of
the Talmud regarding the issue of how words are to be interpreted—i.e.,
whether the text may be read without regard to the traditional vocalization,
thereby proving, as it were, that the Torah itself alludes to the existence of
the cross to which Jacob bowed:[18]

> The apostates say that 'If there is a mother [i.e., authoritative basis] to the
> tradition[al reading],' then one should consider the fact that in the verse
> 'Then Israel bowed at the head of the bed' [Gen. 47:31], the Hebrew word
> for bed (*mittah*) is written without a *yod* and can therefore be read *matteh*,
> which means staff. Consequently, it is probable that it was customary to
> place a cross at the head of dying men, and it was to the cross that Jacob
> bowed.[19]

The convert likewise makes use of his knowledge of the manner in which
one ought to write a Torah scroll, according to which there are certain
letters that are written in a larger form than others—e.g., in Deuteronomy
32:6, in the phrase *Ha la-Shem tigmelu zot*, in which the letter *Heh* (which has
a numerical value of five) is written larger than the other letters. According
to the apostate, this is intended as an allusion to the five wounds of Jesus,
and to his death.

Why is the *heh* of the word *Ha Ladonai* ('Is it to the Lord?') in the phrase,

'Is it to the Lord that you requite this?' [Deut. 32:6] written large? It must refer to the five (*heh*) wounds that you inflicted upon the hanged one.[20]

The author notes that the apostates make use of a typical midrashic method in order to attach verses to one another, to create a message that supports Christianity:

A certain apostate said: It is written 'For it is your life and longevity' [Deut 30:20]; thus the Torah is called life. It is also written, 'And your life shall be hung before you' [Deut. 28:26]—this refers to the fact that the hanged one is life.[21]

Some primary sources also deal with the fact that former apostates lived in the same communities as members of the Jewish group. The severe attitude towards the apostates and the hostility towards the act of conversion may be seen in the language and images by which they are described in these sources. The use of harsh imagery in internal Jewish texts to attack explicitly Christian symbols, such as Jesus, churches, etc., is a specifically Jewish response.[22] The discussion below will focus on this imagery in connection with the ceremony of conversion, baptism, and especially the instrument of conversion—water. More than anything else, the ceremony of baptism characterizes the creation of the new Christian, whether as an infant entering the world of Christian belief or an adult being baptized as a Christian.[23] In the Jewish descriptions of the First Crusade written in the first half of the twelfth century in Germany and northern France, and in Jewish apologetics written in the thirteenth century, such as *Sefer Yosef ha Mekane* and *Sefer Nizzahon Vetus*, the baptismal water, the ultimate Christian symbol, is always described as dirty, foul smelling, disgusting, and evil. More than anything else, these epithets express what the authors sought to impart to their readers about the process of conversion to Christianity.[24]

Although the Jews looked upon this, as well as other Christian ceremonies, with great skepticism, they had to deal with several complex theological issues in connection with it. The Christians in the time of Justin Martyr find support for the ceremony of baptism in the Bible, where immersion is regarded as a means of absolution from sins, and in which two miracles happen to the people of Israel in connection with water: the parting of the Red Sea and the crossing into the Land of Israel via the River Jordan. Both *Sefer Yosef ha Mekane* and *Nizzahon Vetus* deal with the Christian perception of the Israelites' crossing of the Red Sea as the baptism of the Jews. The basis for this notion is found in the Augustinian image that views the Christians as persecuted by sin until they are baptized and cleansed, just as the Egyptians pursued the Israelites until they became baptized as they crossed the Red Sea. As noted by the author of *Nizzahon Vetus*: 'Here the heretics say that all Israel was baptized in the sea in accordance with their impure practice.' Furthermore, the Christians note that it was not Moses who brought the Israelites into the Land of Israel, but Joshua who led them across the River Jordan. The Christians use this biblical episode to persuade the Jews of the power of baptism under the leadership of Joshua/Jesus. This is even more significant as the main element of Moses' legacy, circumcision, was eliminated from that of Joshua/Jesus, whose main symbol is baptism.[25]

The Jewish interpretations, which attempted to refute this Christian proof, rejected the notion that the crossing of the Red Sea and Jordan were acts of baptism. *Sefer Yosef ha Mekane* caustically notes that those saved in the Red Sea had walked on dry land, whereas those who got wet (he uses the term 'became defiled in the water'!), died. He even takes advantage of the Christian image claiming that the rescue of the Israelites in the Red Sea was proof that the Jewish people would be saved from their present situation as well: 'We will live among you and not become sullied with water'—an obvious allusion to Jews who had converted to Christianity and 'become sullied' by baptism. The Jewish apologist also asserts that Jesus and John the Baptist were circumcised, and that any Christian who claims that baptism has replaced circumcision according to Jesus ignores what is stated in the New Testament itself, in Matthew 5:17—i.e., that Jesus had not come to detract from the Torah. To reinforce his views against the Christian ceremony of baptism, the polemicist cites the image of David who prays: 'Save me, O God, for the waters are come in even unto the soul' (Psalms 69:2). In this psalm, King David himself prays against the Christians in order to help the Jews who were being forced by them to become baptized.[26]

The Jewish sources go on to reject the Christian notion that all biblical references to purification by water are an allusion to baptism, as interpreted by Jesus. First, they are careful to reject this idea on a theological basis, pointing out that it does not even make any sense. Second, they use a contemptuous tone towards this explicitly Christian symbol, transforming it from an embodiment of grace, pity, and new life to a representation of larceny, murder, and impurity. In one example, based on the similarity between the Hebrew words for 'wine' and 'drunkard' (סבא/סובא), a comparison is drawn between Isaiah 1:21–22, which mentions 'wine mixed with water,' and Deuteronomy 21:20, which speaks of the son who is sentenced to death for being a 'glutton and drunkard.' The baptismal waters are looked upon with the same contempt as the son, i.e., the 'wine mixed with water.' 'Here, behold how loathsome *shemad* (forced conversion) is to the Lord, as He has made it more contemptible than murder and thievery.' Thus, a person who accepts the baptismal waters is tantamount to having assumed the status of murderer, glutton, and drunkard.[27]

The excesses of the drunken and gluttonous son are described in the exegeses of the twelfth and thirteenth century as lusts leading to the appetite for murder. The baptismal water, the sublime Christian symbol which comes to purify and to renew, is given an extremely negative interpretation among the Jews and is referred to in contemptuous terms of cheapness, ugliness, filth, and contamination; 'the water of stench,' 'the stain of their baptism,' 'the well of Gehinnom,' 'the raging waters,' and 'immersion in the abominable water.' In one passage, alluding to Jeremiah's words upon the water, the author of *Nizzahon Vetus* compares the baptismal water to waters that are 'stagnant, stinking'—i.e., waters that cannot serve in Judaism for any matter of purity. The symbol of water is perceived in such a negative fashion by a twelfth-century French commentator, R. Yitzhak of Troyes, who claims that the reason the phrase 'it was good' is not said on the second day of creation, in contrast to all the other days, is because this day deals entirely with water.[28]

In the polemical literature, the apostate articulates an aggressive position to his brethren, who have remained Jewish even on the simplest levels, indicating in a deep way his own treachery. Rabbi Nathan, in his book *Sefer Yosef ha Mekane*, is forced to refute the claim of the apostate that the Jews are uglier than the Christians. On the superficial level, the author of this work hints that this Jew converted because he was jealous of the beauty of the Christians. On the deeper level, we have here a complex psychological perception that suggests feelings of true inferiority in this area, for the author of the responsum accepts the statement of the apostate, which he interprets in various ways.[29]

Why did such an extreme attitude take hold in relation to the convert to Christianity? Were these merely theological conclusions in light of the growing phenomenon of conversion to Christianity?

Towards the end of the twelfth century the attitude towards apostates changed, corresponding to the changing legal position of the Church, particularly as there began to appear a new type of apostate—one who caused harm to the Jewish community from which he came. At the beginning of the twelfth century Emperor Henry IV allowed those Jews who had been forced to be baptized to return to Judaism. This was perceived in an extremely negative light in the eyes of the Church, and in the middle of the twelfth century Pope Alexander III explicitly forbade it. From 1201 on, a new and different attitude emerged in relation to those who converted to Christianity in the wake of Pope Innocent III's activity regarding this question.[30] Innocent effectively defined an approach that prevented one who had been baptized from returning to his previous situation, and even improved the status of the convert to Christianity by stating that it was desirable that he be in a better position than before (i.e., as a Jew), allowing the apostate to keep the property he had acquired as a Jew. From that point on, the Jewish convert to Christianity did not necessarily lose his property, and was not impoverished and dependent upon the compassion of others. From the end of the twelfth century, and particularly during the thirteenth, the French and English kings were more influenced by this approach than they were by the need to protect the Jews living in their territory, and there developed an increasingly strict attitude towards the return of apostate Jews, even those converted by force, to the Jewish world. In 1267, the papal bull *Torbato Corde* brought this tendency to its height. However, one should note that in England this tendency had already led, in the 1230s, to the first royal organization that was 'concerned' as to what happened to these Jews after their conversion to Christianity. From the time of Henry III, and throughout the reign of Edward I, there was an established policy to house Jews who converted, and to support them economically at the expense of the kingdom—albeit the money for this purpose was taken directly from the former Jews, and used to finance them once they were Christians. This new activity of the English crown was certainly known to the Jewish leadership in northern France (most of whom were related to the families of English Jewry), and almost certainly to the Jews of Germany.[31]

From the mid-twelfth century on a new kind of apostate appears, one who causes direct harm to the Jewish community to which he had belonged. We first learn of this phenomenon in a story related in *Mahzor Vitry*. The Capatian king (evidently Louis VII) called upon R. Moshe ben Yehiel ben Matityah of Paris, asking him whether it was true that when Jews bury their dead they perform magical acts and curse the Christians in a ceremony that consisted of throwing dirt and grass. The king derived this information from the words of Jewish apostates. R. Moshe explained the Jewish custom as an innocent belief pertaining to the Resurrection of the Dead, a belief based upon the verse in Psalms: 'May there be abundance of grain in the land; on the tops of mountains may it wave; may it be like Lebanon; and may men blossom from the cities like the grass of the field' (Psalms 72:16), and that under no circumstance was it intended to harm Christians. In his reply,

R. Moshe made use of a verse from Psalms, a book particularly close to the hearts of Christians, and of a verse whose interpretation could be accepted even by the strictest Christian. By this he exposed the apostate's scheme to mislead the king and to harm the Jews, his loyal subjects. According to the Jewish source, the king praised the Jewish custom and was shocked by the act of the apostate, to the extent that he cursed him severely: 'More power to you, and well do you do. This is a great and good belief, for you are a holy people to your God. Cursed be those who slander you, for they do not know the goodness of your faith, for this is all of man's [duty].'[32] The author's view is clear. He distinguishes a new type of apostate, who seeks to harm his former group, emphasizing this by placing words of curse and imprecation in the mouth of the Christian king. The curse emphasizes (according to the Jewish prayer, the *Amidah*) the emergence of slanderers, whose existence makes the curse necessary.

The problem of harmful apostates was exacerbated during the thirteenth century with the appearance of Nicholas Donin de la Rochelle. Donin was a Jewish apostate who had converted to Christianity, apparently after having been a student in the yeshiva of R. Yehiel of Paris. His central idea was to deny the Jews the Talmud and thereby accelerate their conversion to Christianity. To this end, he wrote a letter in 1236 to Pope Gregory IX with a list of thirty-five accusations against the Talmud, claiming that the purpose of the Talmud was twofold: heresy that changes the understanding of the 'Old Testament,' and concealing the Christian truth from the Jews. On Saturday, 3 March 1239, at the instruction of the pope, all of the books of the Jews in Paris were confiscated in order to examine whether they were indeed heretical. A trial was conducted for the Talmud and three of the senior Jewish leaders in Paris, headed by R. Yehiel of Paris, who was doubtless the most important and strongest figure in the Jewish community there, were called upon to defend it. When the Jewish spokesmen failed to do so, it was declared a heretical book, and sentenced to being burned.[33]

We have an extant source from the thirteenth century describing the 'debate' between the Christian theologians who attacked the Talmud, and R. Yehiel, who defended it.[34] This work is attributed to R. Yehiel, but it is not clear whether it was written by him, his son, one of his students, or, as seems most likely, by R. Yosef ha Mekane. It is clear that it was written after the severe crisis described above in which the Jews lost the basis for their religious life and for their self-definition with the burning of the Talmud, which created a need to write a book that would strengthen the Jews so as to withstand the Christians. The beginning of *Sefer ha-Vikuah* is devoted to a denunciation and rejection of this apostate. Nicholas Donin is cursed and condemned, and it is emphasized that he is classified as an evildoer—'the name of the wicked shall rot'; it is wished that he not have any offspring; his descendants are also accursed. He is referred to there as 'Haman,' 'a foolish person,' 'one who breaks the boundaries,' 'a serpent,' 'a sinner,' 'she-ass,' 'enemy,' 'may his shame be increased, that he brought our dispute to the king and to his council.' In other words, as they understood matters, an apostate had appeared whose purpose was to deprive Jews of the Talmud, to denounce the Jews before the Christians in such a manner as to deny them the right to dwell in the place and the ability to conduct their lives, and to judge them according to the Talmud. The abundance of terms of opprobrium indicates they no longer saw him as a 'brother.'

Another convert to Christianity who greatly worsened the situation of the Jews in France was Pablo Christiani, a Jew from Montpellier who was born with the name Saul in 1210. He received a regular Jewish education, was familiar with Talmud and midrashim, was married to a Jewish woman, and was a father of children. He converted to Christianity at the beginning of the 1230s and joined the Dominican order (Order of Preaching Friars); he left his wife, took his children, and converted them as well.[35] Friar Pablo's main activity with the Dominican order was in Spain, in connection with the public polemic conducted against R. Moses Nahmanides (Ramban) in Barcelona in 1263 which, both in terms of geographical area and in terms of the problematic involved in the attitude towards apostates, was not similar to that which prevailed in France and Germany.[36] In the wake of the discoveries of Professor Shatzmiller, it has become clear that Friar Pablo made his way to Paris in 1269 where, under the aegis of King Louis IX, he debated with and preached to the Jews regarding the Christian truth.[37] In response to this activity, the Jews wrote a book of polemics for internal purposes, to ensure that Pablo Christiani's arguments would be familiar to the Jews, so that they might effectively confront them and defend themselves against them. This book was similar to that written after the crisis caused by Donin twenty-five years earlier. The author describes Pablo's manner of activity with great anger, and particularly the nature of his arguments, which are reminiscent of those Nahmanides had to deal with in Barcelona in 1263. He was particularly angry because Pablo was so familiar with the Jewish way of life; he was expert, not only in the *aggadah* and the Talmud, but even describes the bodily gestures used by Jews during prayer.[38]

But this Hebrew book reveals something else beyond the theological debate. From the Jewish point of view, Pablo represented numerous and threatening dangers. The Jews compare him to Donin: like him he is an apostate, and he also protested against the Jews in the days of Rabbi Yehiel of Paris. Just as in the ancient period there were scribes whose function was to write so that people would know how to answer an *apikorus* (according to *b. Sanhedrin* 38b), so too they write against Pablo, who is referred to on only one occasion as a *meshumad*, and more generally as *min* or *kofer* ('heretic').[39]

The Jews emphasize that the aim of this apostate was the destruction of the Jews and not their conversion. According to them, this apostate, a Dominican monk, argued that the Jews as a whole are responsible for the murder of Jesus, a claim whose purpose is the destruction of the Jews, 'and one who is knowledgeable should be very reluctant to speak about the murder of Jesus, because this one [i.e., Pablo] revealed that it is his intention to destroy all the Jews.'[40] Moreover, according to them Pablo emphasizes that the Jews have no right to defend their religion because they are *bougres* of fire: that is to say, literally, heretics, who are subject to death by fire. Pablo speaks decisively against those Christians who are tolerant of the Jews, for as heretics they need to be burned. In other words, this is not at all a religious debate, but preaching intended to destroy them. The Hebrew text contains more than a hint of the great danger in the connection between the apostate and the king, who listens to him and states that the 'heresy' of the Jews is worse than 'idolatry.'[41] The author notes that Pablo received an order from the king so that, whenever he wishes to debate the Jews, all the Jews, 'great and small,' must appear at the command of the king to listen to him. The example given is the description of the gathering of all the Jews of Paris in the Dominican courtyard at Rue San Jacques in Paris,[42] while opposite a large Christian crowd Pablo began to describe Jesus' murder by the Jews by stabbing and hanging.

In the middle of the thirteenth century, the Jews experienced the emergence of a new type of convert to Christianity, one in the vanguard of the Christian theological struggle against Judaism, who reveals 'secrets' and knowledge from the Jewish world of the past in support of Christianity in order to destroy Judaism from its foundations.

Notes

1 S. Goldin, *The Ways of Jewish Martyrdom*, Turnhout 2008, pp. 190–192.

2 I. Davidson, *Thesaurus of Medieval Jewish Poetry* [Hebrew], 4 vols. New York 1970, Vol. 1, p. 129, No. 2, 745; A. Grossman, 'Saladin's Victory and the Aliya of the Jews of Europe to the Land of Israel,' *Studies in the History of Eretz Israel, Presented to Yehuda Ben Porat*, eds. Y. Ben-Arieh and E. Reiner, Jerusalem 2003, pp. 361, 381.

3 *Midrasch Tehillim (Midrash on Psalms)*, ed. S. Buber, Wilna 1892 [repr. Jerusalem 1966], Psalm 28, s.v. [2].

4 Davidson, *Thesaurus*, Vol. 1, p. 129, No. 2, 745.

5 Davidson, *Thesaurus*, Vol. 1, p. 129, No. 2, 745.

6 Ya'akov ben Meir, *Sefer ha-Yashar* (Responsa), ed. S. Rosenthal, Berlin 1918, Nos. 25–26, pp. 42–45, and No. 93, p. 74; Ya'akov ben Meir, *Sefer ha-Yashar* (News), ed. S. Schlesinger, Jerusalem 1959, pp. 448–449; Tosafot *Gittin* 34b s.v. *veho* (והוא); J. Katz, *Exclusiveness and Tolerance*, Oxford 1961, pp. 67–68; E. E. Urbach, *The Tosaphists: Their History, Writings and Methods*, Jerusalem 1980, p. 121; A. Grossman, *The Early Sages of France* [Hebrew], Jerusalem 1995, p. 503; Judah b. Samuel he-Hasid, *Sefer Hasidim*, ed. J. Wistinetzki, Frankfurt am Main 1924, p. 74, No. 193.

7 B. Blumenkranz, 'Jüdische und Christliche Konvertiten im jüdisch-christlichen Religions gespräch des Mittelalters,' in: *Judentum im Mittelalter: Beiträge zum christlich-jüdischen Gespräch*, ed. P. Wilpert, Berlin 1966, pp. 264–283; J. Cohen, 'The Mentality of the Medieval Jewish Apostate: Peter Alfonsi, Hermann of Cologne and Pablo Christiani, in: *Jewish Apostasy in the Modern World*, ed. T. M. Endelman, New York 1987, pp. 20–47; A. Saltman, 'Hermann's *Opusculum de conversion sua*: Truth or Fiction?' *Revue des études juives* 147 (1988), pp. 31–56; A. Kleinberg, 'Hermanus Judaeos Opusculum: In Defence of its Authenticity,' *Revue des études juives* 151 (1992), pp. 337–353; J. C. Schmitt, 'La memoire de Premontre: a propos de l'autobiographie du Premontre Herman le Juif,' in: *La vie des moines et chanoines reguliers au Moyen Age et temps modernes*, ed. M. Derwich, Wroclaw 1995, pp. 439–452; A. Haverkamp, 'Baptised Jews in German Lands during the Twelfth Century,' in: *Jews and Christians in Twelfth-Century Europe*, eds. M. Signer and J. Van Engen, Notre Dame, Ind., pp. 279–283; Cohen, 'Between Martyrdom and Apostasy: Doubt and Self-Definition in the Twelfth-Century Ashkenaz,' *Journal of Medieval and Early Modern Studies* 29 (1999), pp. 431–471.

8 Urbach, *The Tosaphists*, pp. 498–499; E. Kupfer, 'A Contribution to the Chronicles of the Family of R. Moses Ben Yom-Tov "the Noble" of London,' [Hebrew] *Tarbiz* 40 (1971), pp. 385–387; H. H. Ben-Sasson, *Continuity and Variety* [Hebrew], Tel Aviv 1984, pp. 61–62; E. Horowitz, 'Medieval Jews Face the Cross,' in: *Facing the Cross*, eds. Y. T. Assis, J. Cohen, A. Kedar et al., Jerusalem 2000, pp. 118–140, at pp. 120–121.

9 W. C. Jordan, 'Adolescence and Conversion in the Middle Ages: A Research Agenda,' in: *Jews and Christians in Twelfth-Century Europe*, eds. M. A. Signer and J. Van Engen, Indiana 2001, pp. 77–93 (esp. pp. 87–93).

10 Grossman, *The Early Sages of France*, pp. 27, and 145ff., notes 138–140. An example not from this region—the Introduction to Yosef Kimhi's *Sefer ha-Berit*, 1105–1170—specifically states that his students asked him to gather proofs from the Torah against the claims of the Christians, to whom he refers as 'schismatics and heretics.'

11 Yosef b. Natan Official, *Sefer Yosef ha Mekane*, ed. J. Rosenthal, Jerusalem 1970, pp. 32, 34 (No. 6); 36 (10), 82 (86), 117 (128), 45 (23), 91 (98), 68 (62), 77 (82), 75 (78), 95 (104).

12 D. Berger, *The Jewish-Christian Debate in the High Middle Ages: A Critical Edition of the Nizzahon Vetus*, introduction, translation, and commentary D. Berger, Philadelphia 1979, pp. 32–37.

13 Berger, *The Jewish-Christian Debate*, pp. 94–95 (No. 78), 206–207 (211), 226–228 (242).

14 Berger, *The Jewish-Christian Debate*, pp. 60–62, 248–252.

15 Berger, *The Jewish-Christian Debate*, pp. 42 and 235, 347–349: 'The apostates may say: Why is the world "God" written in the plural form *Elohim* when it should have been written in the form *Eloah*? Surely it is because there are two, father and son.'

16 Berger, *The Jewish-Christian Debate*, pp. 42–43 (No. 5).

17 Berger, *The Jewish-Christian Debate*, p. 43.

18 In *b. Kiddushin* 18b; *Sanhedrin* 4a–b; *Makkot* 7b.

19 Berger, *The Jewish-Christian Debate*, pp. 59 (No. 26) and 248.

20 Berger, *The Jewish-Christian Debate*, pp. 78 (No. 54) and 275.

21 Berger, *The Jewish-Christian Debate*, p. 58 and see his note on p. 265 (No. 14) for the Christological interpretation of this verse.

22 A. S. Abulafia, 'Invectives against Christianity in the Hebrew Chronicles of the First Crusade,' in: *Crusade and Settlement*, ed. P. W. Edbury, Cardiff 1985, pp. 66–72; Berger, *The Jewish-Christian Debate*, pp. 3–40.

23 P. Cramer, *Baptism and Change in the Early Middle Ages, 200–1150*, Cambridge 1993.

24 A. Habermann, ed., *Sefer Gezerot Ashkenaz ve-Zarfat*, Jerusalem 1945, pp. 25, 36, 38, 39, 42, 87, 97; Berger, *The Jewish-Christian Debate*, pp. 65, 172–175, 325–326; A. S. Abulafia, *Christians and Jews in the Twelfth-Century Renaissance*, London 1995, pp. 70, 154, Nos. 23–24.

25 Yosef b. Natan Official, *Sefer Yosef ha Mekane*, p. 47 s.v. 27. See also *Sefer Nizzahon (Yashan) Vetus*, in Berger, *The Jewish-Christian Debate*, p. 65 s.v. 35 and note p. 254, the list of Christian theologians who wrote about it: Isidore, Bede [pseud.], Raban Maur and p. 226; Abulafia, *Christians and Jews*, pp. 105, 124–125, 164, note 62.

26 Yosef b. Natan Official, *Sefer Yosef ha Mekane*, p. 47; *Sefer Nizzahon (Yashan) Vetus*, in Berger, *The Jewish-Christian Debate*, pp. 172–173, 312–313.

27 Yosef b. Natan Official, *Sefer Yosef ha Mekane*, pp. 73–74. The old French word he uses to define this is '*ta glotonie*' (gluttony). See *Sefer Nizzahon (Yashan) Vetus*, in Berger, *The Jewish-Christian Debate*. Against Christian baptism see paragraphs 51, 63, 157, 160–161 (pp. 77, 171ff., 175–177, 314). See for example ibid., 196, pp. 201, 325–326: 'Gregory interpreted that we should placate our Creator for saving us from the impure water that was sanctified falsely through the god who can be represented by an image.'

28 Berger, *The Jewish-Christian Debate*, p. 85 (No. 64); Grossman, *The Early Sages of France*, p. 504.

29 There is a parallel to this story also in *Nizzahon Vetus*, albeit there, in a more logical way, the question is raised by a Christian rather than by a Jewish convert to Christianity. Yosef b. Natan Official, *Sefer Yosef ha Mekane*, p. 95; *Sefer Nizzahon (Yashan) Vetus*, in Berger, *The Jewish-Christian Debate*, p. 195.

30 Haverkamp, 'Baptized Jews in German Lands,' pp. 264–267, notes 66–68.

31 S. Grayzel, 'Popes, Jews, and Inquisition: From "Sicut" to "Torbato corde,"' in: *Essays on the Occasion of the Seventieth Anniversary of the Dropsie University (1909–1979)*, eds. A. Katsch and L. Nemoy, Philadelphia 1977, pp. 151–188; R. C. Stacey, 'The Conversion of Jews to Christianity in Thirteenth-Century England,' *Speculum* 67 (1992), pp. 263–283.

32 *Mahzor Vitry*, ed. S. Horowitz, Nuremberg 1892, No. 280; Yosef b. Natan Official, *Sefer Yosef ha Mekane*, p. 61 s.v. 49; Urbach, *The Tosaphists*, pp. 46, 140.

33 S. Grayzel, *The Church and the Jews in the XIIIth Century*, rev. edition, New York 1966, pp. 29–33, 240, 250, 275, 341–345; J. M. Rosenthal, 'The Talmud on Trial: The Disputation at Paris in the Year 1240,' *Jewish Quarterly Review* 47 (1956–57), pp. 58–76 and 145–169; C. Merchavia, *The Church Versus Talmudic and Midrashic Literature 500–1248* [Hebrew], Jerusalem 1970, pp. 227–360; J. Shatzmiller, 'Did Nicholas Donin Promulgate the Blood Libel?' [Hebrew] *Mehkarim* 4 (1978), pp. 173–182; C. Merchavia 'Did Nicholas Donin Instigate the Blood Libel?' [Hebrew] *Tarbiz* 49 (1980), pp. 11–121; W. C. Jordan, *The French Monarchy and the Jews: From Philip Augustus to the Last Capetians*, Philadelphia 1989, pp. 137–141.

34 Yehiel ben Joseph, *Vikuah* [Dispute], ed. R. Margulies, Lvov 1928; I. Loeb, 'La controverse de 1240 sur le Talmud,' *Revue des études juives* 1 (1880), pp. 247–261, 2 (1881), pp. 248–270, 3 (1883), pp. 39–57; Y. Baer, 'The Disputation of R. Yehiel of Paris and of Nahmanides,' [Hebrew] *Tarbiz* 2 (1931) pp. 172–187; R. Chazan, 'The Condemnation of the Talmud Reconsidered (1239–1248),' *PAAJR (Proceedings of the American Academy for Jewish Research)* 55 (1988), pp. 11–30.

35 Cohen, 'The Mentality of the Medieval Jewish Apostate,' pp. 35–40; J. Cohen, *The Friars and the Jews*, Ithaca 1982, pp. 108–128.

36 Y. Baer, *A History of the Jews in Christian Spain*, 2 vols. Philadelphia 1961, 1966, Vol. 1, pp. 152–159; R. Chazan, *Medieval Jewry in Northern France*, Baltimore 1973, pp. 149–153; J. Cohen, *Friars and Jews*, pp. 108–128; R. Chazan, 'From Friar Paul to Friar Raymond: The Development of Innovative Missionizing Argumentation,' *Harvard Theological Review* 73 (1983), pp. 289–306.

37 J. Shatzmiller, *La deuxième controverse de Paris: un chapitre dans la polemique entre Chretiens et Juifs au Moyen Age* (Collection de la REJ, 15), Paris 1994; R. Chazan, *The Jews of Medieval Western Christendom 1000–1500*, Cambridge 2006, pp. 251–252.

38 Shatzmiller, *La deuxième controverse de Paris*, p. 50 and note 103.
39 Shatzmiller, *La deuxième controverse de Paris*, pp. 36, 37.
40 Shatzmiller, *La deuxième controverse de Paris*, p. 60.
41 Shatzmiller, *La deuxième controverse de Paris*, p. 22 and note 26; J. Shatzmiller, 'The Albigensian Heresy as Reflected in the Eyes of Contemporary Jewry,' in: *Culture and Society in Medieval Jewry*, eds. M. Ben-Sasson, R. Bonfil, and J. Haker, Jerusalem 1989, pp. 333–352; J. Cohen, 'The Second Disputation of Paris and Its Place in Thirteenth Century Jewish Christian Polemic,' [Hebrew] *Tarbiz* 68 (1999), pp. 557–579.
42 In Shatzmiller's translation: 'dans l'enclos de l'institution de la maison des Jacobins,' *La deuxième controverse de Paris*, p. 56.

4

Self-definition and halakhah

The halakhic definition of Jewishness is one of the prime factors fashioning the Jew's understanding both of himself and of his environment. The halakhic attitude towards those Jews who voluntarily embraced Christianity, or who were forced to accept that religion, shaped the disposition of those Jews who remained Jews as against those who became Christians. While the halakhic literature contains decisions deriving, by and large, from explicitly halakhic considerations, it also reflects changes in stance and in historical and sociological valuations, as well as reactions to popular views and feelings towards those who had abandoned the Jewish religion and chose to live within the Christian world. From the twelfth century on, there is substantive difficulty in arriving at a clear halakhic decision regarding the issue of those who became Christians. To people of that time, the earlier, inclusive approach of Rashi seemed excessive, but neither did they wish to explicitly state that they had given up hope of the apostates' return to Judaism. The view that remains holds that the position of those who hesitate whether or not to return to Judaism must not be weakened, coupled with the consideration that, from a propaganda viewpoint, it was important to leave a spark of hope in the hearts of those who remained Jews so that they not see the conversion of Jews to Christianity as a success of Christian theology, because those Jews would also sooner or later return to the fold. The halakhic writings relate to numerous questions presented for discussion to those authorities, either sitting as Rabbinic judges or responding to queries addressed to them. Their halakhic responses thus reflect their approaches to what was taking place around them, their reaction to increasingly frightening historical events, and their attitude towards the Christian environment. Their writings likewise reflect the popular perceptions within their communities, which they needed to deal with when writing their halakhic decisions.

The subjects discussed are numerous and complex. Some of them relate to perennial questions, frequently discussed, such as matters of personal status (divorce and levirate marriage), interest, and inheritance. However, new questions also arise, concerning both the halakhic subject matter and issues of self-definition. Should one mourn for an apostate who has died or for his son, and how? Should one accept an apostate who wishes to return to Judaism, and if so how? These issues pertain to the identity and self-definition of the Jew who remained a Jew despite all difficulties. The general attitude was that the graver the overall position of the Jews, the more Christianity seemed to be victorious and, in particular, the more the 'apostates' came to be seen as dangerous and harmful to the Jewish group, and the stricter the halakhah was with the 'apostate.'

The deterioration in the attitude towards converts to Christianity, in contrast with that of Rabbenu Gershom Meor ha-Golah and Rashi, began in the middle of the twelfth century, once the second generation following the First Crusade had internalized the substantive change undergone by the Christian world. During the first half of the twelfth century, they had been able to assume that the definitions of the previous generation still held.

During the first half of the twelfth century, we find Rabbi Eliezer ben Nathan (Ra'avan) still underscoring Rashi's assertion that it is forbidden to take interest from a convert as he is considered a brother despite his conversion to Christianity: that is, his Jewish essence remains unchanged. Ra'avan adds that it is also forbidden to sell him non-kosher meat, due to the prohibition 'you shall not place an obstacle before a blind person': in other words, he looks upon the Christian convert as one whose Jewish essence has not changed, even though he has changed his religion.[1]

This approach changed, however, in both France and Germany once we cross the mid-century mark. It may be that the events of the Second Crusade, although they did not affect the Jews in the same way the First Crusade had, finally made it clear to the Jews that a change had taken place.

Northern France

Rabbenu Tam (Rabbi Ya'akov ben Meir; d. 1171), who reflects the generation of the second half of the twelfth century, allowed a convert to Christianity who wished to return to Judaism to do so in a straightforward and simple manner, without untoward difficulties; nevertheless, his overall attitude towards such Jews was very strict. Until then, it had not occurred to the

leadership that one ought to require a Christian convert who wished to
return to undergo a ceremony tantamount to that required of a proselyte
to Judaism, as the apostate to Christianity had in essence remained a Jew.[2]
R. Yaakov ben Mordechai, his student during the second half of the twelfth
century, expressed astonishment at Rabbenu Tam, ruling regarding a
female apostate to Christianity. His teacher had allowed her to return to
Judaism and to remain married to a Gentile (who had meanwhile converted
to Judaism) with whom she had lived during her apostasy. He attacked the
weak points of Rabbenu Tam's ruling from a halakhic perspective, but it
seems clear that his opposition was based on the view that it was improper
to 'give a prize' to one who had converted to Christianity, even if she
thereby caused a Gentile Christian to embrace Judaism.[3] If, during the first
half of the twelfth century we find questions relating to the possibility of
requiring the returning convert to undergo ceremonies and procedures
intended for the proselyte, such as immersion in *mikveh* or appearance before
a court of three people, from this point on we find halakhic discussions of
the matter from which it becomes clear that the debate was not a strictly
halakhic one, but one that related to the very basis of the self-definition
of the Jew: i.e., the comparison between one who remained Jewish and
one who had left the group.[4] If, previously, the convert to Christianity
had been referred to using the Talmudic term 'a convert out of appetite'
(*mumar le-te'avon*), implying that he was still considered a brother whom one
was required to 'sustain in life,' the halakhic writers now used the term
'a convert out of spite' (*mumar le-hakh'is*), which was tantamount to the
term *meshumad* ('apostate'), thereby changing both the definition and the
implied attitude. The 'apostate,' who is a 'heretic out of spite,' has removed
himself from brotherhood with the Jewish group; hence, there is no reason
to 'sustain his life,' there is no sense of kinship or 'brotherhood,' and it is
permitted to take interest from him. Rashi's grandson, Rabbenu Ya'akov
Tam, explains that the converts of his time are to be seen under the rubric
of *min* ('heretic'; see *b. Avodah Zarah* 26b), such that there is no obligation
to worry about them from an economic viewpoint, and one applies to them
the rule 'one pushes him down and does not raise him up' (that is to say:
if he fell into a pit, one does not help him to get out of there). Hence, he
concludes that is permissible to loan him (i.e., the apostate or the son of an
apostate woman) money on interest.[5]

Rabbenu Tam's theological approach is particularly striking regarding
the question of what rule is to be applied to the Jew who converted to
Christianity, did not return to Judaism, and died as a Christian. The
question raised is whether his relatives are required to mourn for him

as one would for a Jew who died as a sinner, or whether he is defined according to his end: thus, if he died as a Christian, he is considered as a Christian, so that there is no obligation to mourn for him. And what is the law regarding the small child of a convert to Christianity, who was baptized without his consent and died as a Christian? R. Tam and his disciples (R. Yitzhak and R. Yitzhak ben Abraham: Ritzb'a), who lived in the second half of the twelfth century, stated that one does not mourn for them. It would seem that in this case the anger against the apostate, expressed in the absolute refusal to mourn for him, derives from the fact that they were ready to be lenient with him and to accept him back during his lifetime. As we noted, Rabbenu Tam made it possible for a woman who had converted, was divorced by her Jewish husband, and married a Gentile, to return to Judaism together with him. Rabbenu Tam's nephew, R. Yitzhak, permits the use of wine that had been touched by an apostate who claimed to have returned to Judaism 'within himself.' R. Yitzhak's disciple, the Ritzb'a, emphasizes the importance and even urgency of the return to Judaism of the apostate, and attempts to make matters easier for him. He is thus prepared to accept him back as a Jew even if he did not immerse himself in *mikveh*, even if he did not appear before three kosher witnesses to declare his return, and even if he did not abandon his former acts.[6] However, their halakhic decision was that the convert to Christianity who did not exploit the possibility of repentance and died as a Christian is not to be mourned as a Jew. That is, in terms of self-definition, they refused to accept that a Jew who did not stand up to the test, or was convinced by Christianity, was equal to one who remained a Jew. Moreover, when Rabbenu Tam was asked as to whether one is required to mourn for a small child who died after his parents had changed their and his religion, and who of course did not know or understand the significance of the conversion—in his words, 'a child who had been placed in the water, what difference does it make? Shall he not be as if he had never become an apostate?'—he stated that, not only is one not to mourn for an apostate who died, but one is not even to mourn for a small child whose parents converted his religion when he was a child and who died as a child. Had he not died, he would have survived and lived as a Christian; therefore, if he died, not only does one not mourn him, but 'one rejoices over his death more than over his life.' Thus Rabbenu Tam establishes the halakhic boundaries which a Jew may not cross, by which they define themselves as Jews or as 'non-Christians.'[7]

This change found further expression in the 1180s and 1190s. R. Yitzhak established the attitude towards Christianizers on the basis of his disillusionment with the Christian world and the historical developments around him. R. Yitzhak (d. 1175 or 1178) indicates the new boundaries after the incident at Blois (1171), the beginning of the Capetian monarchy synthesis, and the expulsion of the Jews from the royal domain during the reign of Philip II (1182). The local ruler is no longer the absolute protector of the Jews living within his domain, but is influenced by Christian folk attitudes and by those of the Church, which have growing influence. The event in Blois in 1171 clarified the connection between the rulers, the ecclesiastical establishment, and monastic factors playing upon popular sentiment, with fatal results for the Jews, and particularly for Jewish children. In the incident at Blois the Jewish community as a whole was blamed for the murder of a Christian; their guilt was proven through trial by ordeal, they were executed by burning at the stake, and the Jewish children were taken to be raised as Christians.[8] Every Jewish leader in northern France (and even in Germany) after the 1170s was aware of this event, and R. Yitzhak, although he did not respond to the event directly, was well aware that the Christians were interested in converting Jews to Christianity and took active steps to do so. Therefore, even though he did not object to Jews making use of Christian physicians, he forbade leaving small children in the homes of Christians for purposes of healing out of fear that 'they would draw them towards heresy.'[9]

R. Yitzhak, at the end of the twelfth century, already feared the victory of Christianity, and was therefore strict with a Jew who had converted to Christianity, imposing upon him as a test the obligation of a ceremonial immersion in the event of the return to Judaism. As has been demonstrated recently by Kanarfogel, those approaches that basically saw a Jew who had converted to Christianity as remaining a Jew from the Jewish viewpoint did not require that he immerse himself should he wish to return to Judaism, as there is no halakhic logic justifying such a requirement.[10] This stance was approved by the Sages, both those in Germany and in France (including the disciples of R. Yitzhak), as it repeatedly provided a basis for the halakhic view that the connection between one born Jewish and his Judaism cannot be severed. However, in the case of R. Yitzhak, we can discern a new approach being taken towards the convert to Christianity: one that locates the problem in the concrete political realm by attempting to draw a distinction between the Jew who remains a Jew and the one who went astray, thereby strengthening the self-image of the Jew who stubbornly adheres to his Jewishness. The return to Judaism of one who had converted to Christianity seemingly ought to have been a joyful event, one that strengthens those Jews who remained Jews, but R. Yitzhak exploited such occasions as an opportunity to sharpen the distinction between former apostates and those Jews who had maintained their Judaism all along, thereby strengthening their own self-perception. In his eyes, Christian baptism is not simply a pagan ritual, but an imposition of theological authority. The Jew who converts to Christianity is 'considered as a Gentile,' literally—that is, there is Gentile authority over him. Thus, the Jewish community must see that a change has taken place, and that the 'Gentile' authority which had imposed its force upon this individual when he was baptized as a Christian has been removed by means of the new Jewish immersion. The act of immersion which he proposed (and which thereafter became obligatory) was intended for the Jews; hence, emphasis was placed on former converts needing to undergo immersion upon their return, and the involvement and presence of the Rabbinic Court in the process. In Germany, R. Simhah of Speyer and R. Yitzhak Or Zaru'a treated this immersion with even greater seriousness, and the subject was developed thus until, in the days of R. Meir of Rothenburg (end of thirteenth century), it became an obligation.[11]

R. Yitzhak emphasizes the theological aspect in his discussion of the question of interest in relation to the convert to Christianity, clearly expressing the change in attitude towards the converted Jew as deriving from the nature of the Christianity that he has taken upon himself. As we have seen, the issue of interest is one that touches upon the very roots of the Jewish self-definition due to the biblical verses connecting the prohibition against interest with the concept of Jewish fellowship: 'Do not take from him any interest or increase, but fear your God, that your brother may live with you; Do not lend him your money at interest, nor give him your food for profit'; 'You shall not lend upon interest to your brother, interest on money, interest on victuals, interest on anything that is lent for interest' (Leviticus 25:36–37; Deuteronomy 23:20). If we adhere to the definition of the apostate given by Rashi before the First Crusade, the 'apostate' did not depart from the definition of Israel nor that of brotherhood; hence, it is forbidden to loan or borrow money from him at interest under any circumstance, just as his Jewish essence is not nullified with regard to matters of marriage. But R. Yitzhak is concerned that, were Rashi's approach—i.e., that it is forbidden to loan money to the apostate on interest—to be accepted, the difference between the apostate and those who remained Jewish would be obscured; thus, in the consciousness of those who remained Jews, one who 'sinned' and became a Christian would continue to be perceived as a Jew. At the end of the twelfth century, such a possibility was totally unacceptable. R Yitzhak states that, because the converted Jew is now a Gentile, it is permitted to loan him money at interest. In a responsum by R. Yitzhak devoted to the complex issue of the 'son of a converted woman,' he explains at great length and in great detail his view regarding the difficulties that derive from the special relationship to Jews who converted to Christianity.[12]

He notes that he knows Rashi wrote that it is forbidden to loan money at interest to a converted Jew, but he heard from his father the words of Rabbenu Ya'akov Tam that it is permitted to do so (R. Yitzhak's mother was the sister of Rabbenu Tam, the grandson of Rashi). He did not ask the reason for this position, as it seemed to him to be simple and reasonable. Rabbenu Tam's approach derives from the view that one who converted to Christianity is defined as a 'heretic' (Heb.: *min*; i.e., 'an apostate to idolatry' and not a simple *mumar*), so that those definitions fashioned by Rashi necessarily disappear. As against that, R. Yitzhak brilliantly articulates his own view stemming from the change in the historical situation. In his opinion, in the past the debate derived from concern for his offspring— 'that perhaps the seed of the convert will return to Judaism'—because in the past the apostate was not 'assimilated among the Gentiles.' The previous assumption was that the Jew was forced to embrace Christianity and that his children were likewise in such a situation. He does not know the Torah of Israel, 'and he is not assimilated among the Gentiles'—therefore the Jews are commanded to bring him close to Judaism and to save him, or at least to relate to him in a special way. In R. Yitzhak's view, the situation had altered so that by his own time, at the end of the twelfth century, the situation of the 'apostates' had become substantively different. In his day, those Jews who converted to Christianity are completely Christian, have entirely abandoned Jewish religion, are ensconced within the Christian world, and are totally involved in the Christian cult: 'They are attached to the ways of the nations of the world, and they are considered part of them and are immersed among them; they worship their god and abandon the Torah of Israel completely—such a person is a complete Gentile in every respect, even regarding the matter that one is not required to sustain him in life.' The legitimation that he gives for his opinion is more indicative than anything else. It states in the Talmud that, if a building collapses on the Sabbath and people were buried beneath it, among them an 'apostate,' one is required to desecrate the Sabbath in order to save him, because one assumes that either he or his offspring will return to Judaism and observe many Sabbaths. R. Yitzhak states that, in his own day, there is no chance that the 'apostate' will ever observe Sabbath; hence, in his opinion it is no longer permissible to violate the Sabbath on his behalf.[13]

On the other hand, R. Yitzhak also constructs the Jewish self-definition in his time upon the impossibility of changing the Jewish essence, an essence that does not depend upon the deeds or intentions of the former Jew. It is therefore forbidden to accept a loan on interest from a Jew who has converted to Christianity, comparing this to the prohibition of stealing from him.[14] A distinction is also drawn between a Jew who has willingly converted and one who was forced to do so. It was clear to him that the popular perception did not distinguish between the two: they were careful about not drinking the wine of a forced convert, lest it be considered 'gentile wine,' just as they refrained from drinking the wine of one who had converted willingly. The popular mentality did not distinguish between a Jew who lives as a Christian (even if he had been forced to do so) and participates in the Christian ritual connected with wine, which appears to Jewish eyes as an explicit ritual of idolatry or magic, and that same Jew once he has returned to Judaism. Suspicions regarding the wine of one who has returned to Judaism remained. In a responsum dealing with forced converts who returned to Judaism, the interlocutors attempt to clarify whether one needs to be strict and avoid their wine, 'until they have remained steadfast in their repentance many days and their return [to Judaism] is well-known and public.' R. Yitzhak firmly rejects this approach. When the Jews were Christians, he writes, there was firm basis for avoiding their wine, as they were immersed in the Christian cult, which is idolatrous. But as these Jews had been converted to Christianity forcibly ('because of fear of the sword'), he refers to them as 'sinners of Israel' and not as 'apostates'; hence, if one refrains from drinking their wine even after they have returned to Judaism, this will shame them. There is no reason to even imagine that one must wait a certain time until one is allowed to again drink their wine.[15]

It is interesting to note that these halakhic debates continued during the time of his disciples as well. Two of R. Yitzhak's most prominent disciples at the end of the twelfth century, the two brothers, R. Yitzhak (Ritzb'a) and R. Samson of Sens, the sons of Abraham, continue to discuss this point. The argument between them relates to the attitude towards an apostate who had touched wine, but said that he had repented 'within himself.' The Ritzb'a permitted use of the wine, because he noted that this former apostate behaved like a Jew, even if he had not immersed himself in *mikveh* nor appeared before the Court—'because he left his money pouch unguarded on Shabbat' (i.e., was demonstrably strict about Sabbath observance). 'In all events, he is considered as a repentant, since he has abandoned all idolatrous worship (*tarput*) and returned to his Creator.' Ritzb'a also thinks that the apostate who has returned to Judaism is not required to correct his previous

acts nor to compensate those Jews who had been harmed by them when
he was a Christian prior to his return to Judaism ('somewhat similar to
a Gentile'). His brother R. Samson prohibited the use of such wine, and
emphasized all of the strictures in general.[16]

The Jews were suspicious of the Christian essence which they saw as
being attached to the convert to Christianity and which continued to exert
influence upon him even if he had been coerced, and even if he returned
to Judaism.

Germany

In Germany, too, at the end of the twelfth century and the beginning of
the thirteenth, the spiritual leadership ceased to assert the 'Jewishness' of
converts to Christianity. As in the French arena, so too in Germany the
issue of paying or taking interest from converts to Christianity was subject
to a variety of opinions. There were those who insisted that one neither
borrow from them nor loan them money, but these were the minority of
those who wrote on the subject. The majority held that it was forbidden to
loan them money, but it was permitted to borrow from them. Some defined
them as people whose actions indicated they had removed themselves from
the fellowship of other Jews; therefore it was permitted both to loan and
to borrow them (i.e., at interest). This polemic waged throughout the
twelfth and thirteenth centuries and, even if there was a certain note of
greater strictness towards the end of the thirteenth century, there was no
clear decision.[17] Nevertheless, the overall attitude in Germany is stricter
and the tone far more 'dramatic,' relating primarily to the sin committed
by those who converted to Christianity. Hence, the questions which were
investigated with greater depth were those involving mourning for the
death of such an apostate and the procedure for the return of such an
apostate to Judaism.

Three figures who dealt with this issue at the end of the twelfth and the
beginning of the thirteenth century were Rabbi Eliezer ben Yoel ha-Levi
(Rabya'h – 1140–1240), Rabbi Eleazar of Worms (1160–1230), and Rabbi
Yitzhak ben Moshe of Vienna (Or Zaru'a; 1180–1250). In thirteenth-
century Germany, those who returned to Judaism were required to
perform a public act indicating the purity of their intentions. Rabbi Eliezer
ben Yoel ha-Levi (Rabya'h) required a ceremony in order to formally
accept the one returning to Judaism from his life as a Christian. He was
required to 'pass a razor over his head,' to immerse himself in the waters
of the *mikveh* as if he were a proselyte, and to appear before three people

and declare that he had returned to Judaism. True, the Sages of this period emphasized that these acts were not halakhically required even *ab initio*, and that even if the returning apostate did not do so he was still a Jew. Even Rabbi Simhah of Speyer, during the first half of the thirteenth century, who firmly believed that one who returns to Judaism is required to immerse himself in the *mikveh*—that is, he emphasized the public aspect of his renunciation of Christianity and his return to Judaism—nonetheless admits that failure to do so does not nullify his return to the community. The most important thing is the intention of the repentant together with his accepting suffering ('he must pain himself and undergo bodily sufferings to atone for what he has done'). The fact that R. Simhah of Speyer understands that there is no need for these actions from a purely halakhic viewpoint, but nevertheless requires them, reflects his approach towards the individual who has departed from Judaism. Similarly, a woman who converted to Christianity, gave birth to two children, and has now returned to Judaism with them is required to undergo a substantive public ceremony, entailing immersion in water and appearing before a Rabbinic Court, so as to cleanse herself and them of the contamination of Christianity and give them a new, Jewish persona. During the second half of the thirteenth century there was added the requirement that the Court be present at the immersion, exactly as in the case of a proselyte to Judaism.[18]

Rabbi Eleazar of Worms, who was influenced by pietistic notions of sin and atonement for sin, sees one who converts to Christianity as committing two transgressions—a bodily one and a theological one. He sees the apostate as one who has been tempted by physical desires and appetites: he rejoiced on the festival days of the Christians, ate forbidden foods, and had sexual relations with gentile women. According to this pietistic approach, for whatever sin he committed he needs not only to 'do *teshuvah*' (i.e., repent) and return, but also to accept upon himself 'suffering' for his sins in order to educate himself and not to repeat those transgressions. R. Eleazar of Worms constructed an entire program of acts of atonement intended for the apostate, primarily in the physical realm, corresponding to his pleasure and his arrogance, as well as for the theological deviation he performed while he was a Christian as one 'who denied the essential principles of Judaism, who violated the entire Torah.' From his perspective, repentance is accomplished by the very fact that he now lives as a Jew and that he accepts upon himself the fear of Heaven by reciting *Shema Yisrael* (recited twice daily) with fervor. To atone for the apostate's physical or bodily sins, he demands that he refrain from anything associated with Christianity, priests, or the Church: 'He should not sit together with priests or monks

... he should not derive any benefit from anything that is theirs ... he must distance himself from the door of their homes and from the courtyard of the abominations.'[19] Towards the middle of the thirteenth century, at the end of this process, we find the final formulation of these ideas in the writing of R. Yitzhak ben Moshe Or Zaru'a of Vienna. The act of immersion in water is performed in order to purify oneself after living among the impure: 'All those who return require immersion.' R. Yitzhak ben Moshe, in the wake of his teacher R. Simhah of Speyer, presents Christianity as a source of contamination. Those Jews who maintained their Judaism remain pure of the taint of Christianity, while those who stumbled by accepting the 'deviation' of Christianity and now wish to return to the realms of purity must purify themselves. There is a clear emphasis here on the victory of the Jewish immersion over Christian baptism, but use is also made of Jewish myths related to immersion in water and its power to erase sins.[20]

R. Yitzhak ben Moshe likewise concentrates on material relating to the question of mourning for an apostate who died, and attempts to crystallize it. Surprisingly, he repeats the story connected to the conversion to Christianity of the son of Rabbenu Gershom Meor ha-Golah, emphasizing the tradition (which he had received from R. Samson of Sens) that Rabbenu Gershom did in fact mourn for his Christian son. This story was cited during the thirteenth century, but various explanations are offered for his act in order to emphasize that it was unusual, and that Rabbenu Gershom did so for special reasons, inflicting more pain upon himself over the fact that his son had not sufficed to return to Judaism before his death.[21]

There may have been families that nevertheless sat *shivah* for children who converted to Christianity and subsequently died, as in the case cited above involving Rabbenu Gershom Meor ha-Golah. In order to thoroughly reject this seemingly accepting behavior, two very harsh biblical verses were invoked in order to completely negate mourning for one who died as a Christian. One is Isaiah 66:24: 'And they shall go forth and look on the dead bodies of the men that have rebelled against me; for their worms shall not die and their fire shall not be quenched, and they shall be an abhorrence to all flesh.' This verse is interpreted as referring to those apostates who died in their new religion, for whom no atonement is possible: 'Gehinnom shall be completed, but their [punishment] shall never be completed.' The fundamental Jewish approach sees every Jew who dies as someone for whom one is required to mourn and to rend one's garments because, according to the Talmud, the death of a person and the departure of his soul is compared to a Torah scroll which has been burned. Rashi explains: 'Even the emptiest person in Israel is filled with Torah and mitzvoth.'[22] In the case of a Jew who has converted to Christianity and died, one does not mourn but one even rejoices, as inferred from Proverbs 11:10: 'When it goes well with the righteous the city rejoices; and when the wicked perish there are shouts of gladness.' The apostate is perceived as an evildoer, and if he died in this state there is no cause to mourn for him, but rather one rejoices: 'when the wicked perish there are shouts of gladness.'

It seems evident that, during the mid-thirteenth century, the negative attitude towards the convert to Christianity became exacerbated beyond that of the earlier period. R. Yitzhak ben Moshe of Vienna states that a person who has performed a transgression involving the death penalty, and who died before he managed to repent, is classified as 'one who died in his wickedness' (*b. Sanhedrin* 47a), and one does not mourn for such a person. R. Yitzhak ben Moshe draws the connection between the evildoer and the apostate to Christianity by means of a midrash on Proverbs 11:10: 'When it goes well with the righteous the city rejoices, and when the wicked perish there are shouts of gladness.' This verse creates a distinction between 'the righteous'—i.e., those Jews who remained Jewish and were responsible for one another in all things—and the 'wicked'—namely, the converts to Christianity, who abandon Judaism and are outside the framework of Jewish mutual responsibility. The example he uses is the problematic figure of King Ahab. While King Ahab was a Jewish king, he was a sinner and a negative figure who was engaged in constant confrontation with the prophet Elijah. This negative view of such a sinner was predominant from that point on until the end of the thirteenth century: (Psalms 139:21), 'Whoever departs from the ways of the public and dies, one does not engage with him in anything [i.e., his burial and the preparations], and their relatives wear white and eat and drink and rejoice, for the enemy of the Omnipresent has perished, as said "Shall I not quarrel with those who hate you, O Lord."'[23]

The desire to forego any connection with converts to Christianity is clear during the second half of the thirteenth century in the refusal to accept from the apostate anything intended for the Jewish community. They refused to accept from him money for alms or for the communal poorhouse, and in practice prevented him from maintaining any contact with his former group, relinquishing all contact with him. Particularly striking is the fact that the debate over the apostate's position occurs in the context of the Talmudic discussion which emphasizes that one is permitted to accept sacrifices, voluntary offerings, and vows for the Temple from Gentiles, whereas it is only permitted to accept sacrifices from 'the sinners of Israel' if this process will cause them to return to Judaism. This response on the part of various thirteenth-century figures expresses the sense of frustration with the apostate. One no longer assumes that he will return.[24]

Two figures who shaped the halakhic approach of German Jewry at the end of the thirteenth century had been young students in Rabbi Yehiel of Paris's yeshiva at the time of the great crisis created by the apostate Donin, which led to the burning of the Talmud. Rabbi Meir ben Baruch (Maharam of Rothenburg) expressed his emotional anguish at this event in an impressive liturgical poem, *Sha'ali serufah ba-esh* ('Ask, you who have been burned in fire'), which expresses the sense of pain, despair, and powerlessness that enveloped him as a young man in the face of this catastrophe, involving the burning of the pinnacle of Jewish creativity, and the failure of the esteemed teacher of his generation to protect the Talmud. The feeling of betrayal on the part of the apostate Jew who brought about this disaster is not expressed in this *piyyut*, but is shown in Maharam's halakhic stance, which shaped Jewish consciousness during the second half of the thirteenth century.[25] Rabbi Yedidya ben Israel was also a student in Paris at the time of the burning of the Talmud, as well as being present at the time of the severe attack on the Jews of France during the course of the Shepherds' Crusade in 1251. He thereafter moved to Germany, living in Speyer and Nuremburg, was present at the arrest and death of his colleague Rabbi Meir ben Baruch (Maharam of Rothenburg), and lost his own son, Yisrael, who died as a martyr in 1298. R. Meir's and R. Yedidya's responses serve as a prism through which to understand the attitude towards apostates and forced converts to Christianity at the end of the thirteenth and the beginning of the fourteenth century.[26]

Rabbi Meir of Rothenburg was not happy with 'Jews who became apostates and then returned.' He was suspicious of them and of their intentions. One of the cases with which he dealt involved a woman who had been abandoned by her husband, and whom it was impossible to free of her status due to the testimony of a person who had seen him in France (i.e., thereby providing evidence that he was alive). The witness in question was a Jew who had converted to Christianity and then returned to Judaism, who testified as to what he had seen while he was a Christian. R. Meir rejected his testimony as halakhically unacceptable, and characterized his type as Jews who become Christians, going about from place to place, at times presenting themselves as Jews so as to receive food from the Jews, but in practice intending to steal from them. He refers to such types as 'apostates who had returned, but not wholeheartedly,' 'deceivers,' 'empty people,' 'the worst of the Gentiles,' 'abomination,' 'one who immerses [in order to purify himself] while holding a reptile [i.e., an unclean thing] in his hand,' 'a slave to his appetite.' Due to this panoply of characteristics, he denied his qualification to give testimony.[27]

Like his predecessors, Rabbi Meir of Rothenburg also opines that one does not mourn an apostate who has died. The harsh language which he uses in referring to those who converted to Christianity is particularly striking in its severity. He arrives at his decision from the Talmudic discussion concerning those who were executed by the Court. It is stated in the Talmud that one who was executed by the Rabbinic Court, a punishment reserved for severe transgressions, is not to be mourned, even though he may receive atonement. He infers from this that one does not mourn for an apostate under any circumstances, as he does not merit atonement. The severe expressions used in this connection indicate the extent to which he separates himself and other loyal Jews from them, and the extent to which he defines himself in contradistinction to them: 'The punishment of the wicked in *Gehinnom* [Gehenna, hell] is completed, and theirs is never completed'; 'one is not to mourn for them, but one rejoices and is glad'; 'one does not weep and does not eulogize them.'[28] We have observed that there was a certain problem which arose when a man died without offspring. The brother-in-law, who was needed to release the widow under Jewish law, was an apostate. If he did not agree to perform *halitzah* (the ceremony of releasing the woman), the widow would remain unable to marry or would live in sin (i.e., would enter a halakhically illicit liaison). Proof of this difficulty is found in a responsum by R. Yitzhak ben Moshe Or Zaru'a regarding an attempt to release such a widow based on the approach of the Geonim, mentioned in Chapter 1.[29] During the second half of the thirteenth century, R. Meir of Rothenburg attempted to equate the status of a widow who required release from an apostate brother-in-law to that of one whose prospective *levir* suffered from boils. In such a case, the widow was asked whether she was willing to be married to a man who suffered from a noxious skin disease. If she refused, she was then free to remarry (I shall discuss this responsum at length in the final chapter of this book).

By making the decision dependent upon the opinion of the woman, Rabbi Meir of Rothenburg was able to release her from her legal dependence upon the apostate brother-in-law, and even alluded to the danger that, otherwise, the apostate might catch her as well in his 'gentile' net. Rabbi Meir of Rothenburg was concerned about gentile influences, and therefore decided that even if the widow's late husband had two brothers, the older one being an apostate, he should not perform *halitzah*; rather, she must remain in her state of limbo as an *agunah* and wait for the younger brother to perform the ritual, even if he lived far away in a distant country. The reason given was that 'she has a Jewish *yabam* [brother-in-law].' In a later period we hear of a widow who required *yibbum* (levirate marriage) from an apostate who refused to do so because he was '[an apostate] out of spite and he was pious in his idolatrous ways ... For he stated openly that he did not wish to adhere to the beliefs of the Jews ... and she did receive *halitzah*, but was married to a Jewish man without any release.' That is to say, even in matters of personal status the Rabbis adhered to the earlier approach only on the level of principle—i.e., the apostate continued to be considered a Jew in his essence, but in practice he was distanced further and further away from his Jewish relations. Rabbi Meir of Rothenburg, in his responsum, even cuts those thin ties which Rashi had wished to strengthen regarding the connection between the apostate and his former religion and his family which remained Jewish.[30]

A similar tendency appears in the words of Rabbi Yedidya ben Israel and his contemporaries. He is troubled both by those who become Christians, whether deliberately or under coercion, and by those who chose to return to Judaism. A question from the end of the thirteenth century touched the most sensitive nerves of the Jewish community, at a time when violence against Jews had become a routine matter. Christians attacked the Jewish community and killed some of its inhabitants. Others became Christians, and later testified to what they had seen as Christians. A person (Enoch) who was visiting his parents at the time was murdered together with them, and his sons or nephews were taken captive by Christians who demanded a large sum of money for their release. The dispute relates to the inheritance money of the grandfather. The son's widow argued that, because the grandfather was killed first and her husband only thereafter, she was the lawful heir of his son, her husband, who inherited from his father before he himself was killed. She claimed the right to collect her *ketubah*[31] from this money, arguing that this obligation precedes the inheritance of the grandchildren. Against that, the children's guardian argued that the grandchildren are captive, 'under duress' among the Christians and that this property is needed in order to redeem them. The Rabbinic Court accepted the claim of the widow, which was supported by the testimony of former apostates, rather than that of the orphans' guardian. This decision was then discussed by other sages and Rabbinic judges of the time. The court of Speyer supported the original court's decision; on the other hand, there were three figures who were strongly opposed to it: one anonymous, the second the 'humble' R. Yedidya ben Israel, and the third Rabbenu Asher (known as the Rosh).[32]

This is essentially a legal discussion discussing the question of priority between direct inheritance and collection of the obligation embodied in the *ketubah*, citing Talmudic precedents. However, between the lines we may infer the attitude towards those who preferred to convert to Christianity rather than to die as martyrs. Particularly significant are the words of Rabbi Yedidya. It is impossible for us to know whether he wrote his opinion before, after, or during the course of his mourning for his own son, who died as a martyr.

The respondent opposed the Rabbinic Court's decision to rely upon witnesses who had been Christians at the time that the events in question happened. According to him, it is impossible to accept their testimony, because of the defect of those who converted to Christianity because they feared for their lives. In his opinion, most of the Jews (his phrase is '[all but] one out of a thousand') die as martyrs, for the Sanctification of the Name—'even the empty ones among us.'[33] Even those who convert to Christianity under coercion generally attempt to leave it and return to Judaism as soon as possible. Those Jews who converted to Christianity did not hasten to return to Judaism. Thus, he defines a Jew as one who is willing, even if only a simple person, to die for Kiddush Hashem. Against that, those whom he defines as converts to Christianity are a 'negligible minority,' lower even than those he calls 'empty people.' As for those who do not hasten to return to Judaism, they cannot be referred to as 'coerced' converts but rather as 'those who began under coercion, and end up doing so willingly'; hence, he classifies them as 'apostates out of appetite,' who according to the Talmud are disqualified from testifying. He also asks to find reliable witnesses who can testify to these former apostates' behavior during the period when they were Christians.[34]

As it was impossible to completely ignore the precedent established by Rashi as to the acceptance of testimony of forced converts, this author states that it needs to be clear to the judges that these coerced converts in fact behaved secretly as Jews even while in Christian captivity, 'and that they are not suspected of performing transgressions beyond that which the Gentiles forced them to willfully violate.' If this condition is not fulfilled, one may not accept their testimony as to what they saw at that time, despite the fact that they subsequently returned to Judaism. He suspects them of behaving improperly during the time of their captivity as Christians and writes: '[And behold,] in our sins there were a number of coerced converts who admitted that they had relations with menstruant women, and there were a number of people who returned thereafter who were coerced to testify to things which they did not see.' In other words, Enoch's widow must bring witnesses to make it clear that these people behaved as Jews in captivity, and only then can they testify to what they saw. Beyond his desire to give preference to the release of the children being held captive among the Christians over the inheritance of the widow, it is clear that in principle he viewed those Jews who converted to Christianity, even if done under coercion, in a negative light and cast doubt upon the sincerity of their wish to return to Judaism. According to his view, one may not accept their testimony regarding who had been killed first and to whom the inheritance goes. His goal is clear, and he does not conceal it: he wishes to see the money transferred in such a way that it will help to free the children from the hands of the Christians rather than to give it to the widow on the strength of her *ketubah*, which is ordinarily the strongest note of indebtedness. In terms of his self-definition as a Jew, he provides a basis for what was generally accepted at the end of the thirteenth century—namely, that a Jew is someone who refrains from converting to Christianity at any cost, one who does not mix with the Christian public, one who does not 'have sexual relations with menstruants' (i.e., improper sexual behavior), and is not an evildoer. Only such a Jew can be a reliable witness.

The Jewish perception of the convert to Christianity was related to an enlightened understanding of the ongoing developments in Christianity. Even if this is barely cited in the halakhic responses regarding the attitude towards the convert to Christianity, these matters are clearly present in the background. The question of the inheritance of the apostate was an important and interesting test case, one through which it is possible to emphasize and to exemplify this perception. During the eleventh century, Rashi underscored that the apostate does not inherit from his relatives, notwithstanding the view that sees in principle one who has converted to Christianity as nevertheless a Jew.[35] This self-evident approach, intended to punish one who had abandoned his religion and to deprive him of property and of financial success, echoes the eleventh-century Christian perception. Christianity saw one who had abandoned the Jewish religion and converted to Christianity as one who had cast off his filthy garments, cleansed himself in water, and been reborn. In this theoretical-idealistic theological perception, the property that had been accumulated by the Jew prior to his conversion to Christianity was part of the filth that was attached to his 'Jewishness.' Property that had been accumulated through loaning money on interest and the sin of usury needed to be left behind in the world of his past. This theological approach fit well the inclination of the rulers (emperors, kings, and princes) in those areas in which Jews lived. It is clear that the kings and princes wished this money to remain in Jewish hands, specifically, because it was thereby subject to the rule or control of the Christian rulers and their needs, and would also continue to earn profit while invested in interest-bearing loans—which would have been impossible had the money passed over to the hands of new Christians. At this stage, the kings and the emperor answered the request of the Jews and legislated that 'just as he leaves the law of his fathers, so he must leave his inheritance behind.'[36]

But during the second half of the twelfth century, a new tendency began to take shape. It became clear to the popes that those Jews who had taken the most significant step from the viewpoint of the Church and converted to Christianity became impoverished and downtrodden Christians, full of despair. Pope Alexander III protested to the archbishops of Spain that the property of Jews who had converted to Christianity passed over to those of their relatives who remained, and was thereby effectively confiscated. While this letter was sent to Spain, this was essentially the situation throughout Europe. In 1169, the pope was forced to intervene in the destiny of a convert to Christianity known as Peter, whose complaint reached as high as the pope. This individual had been baptized in the church of St. Peter in Rheims, whose Mother Superior promised him money for his sustenance (*praebenda*). After her death, the archbishop of the city nullified everything that had been promised him. Similarly, in the city of Tournai a certain Jew converted after being promised a basic stipend, the office of deacon in the church, and a seat in the church choir. The bishop of Tournay tried to evade these promises, an act for which he was subject to severe and extreme rebuke by the pope. For that reason, Pope Alexander III decided to establish a fixed law in this matter in the framework of decisions of the Third Lateran Council of 1179, as follows:

> If, moreover, with God's inspiration, anyone became a convert to Christianity, he shall under no condition be deprived of his property. For converts ought to be in a [sic] better circumstances than they had been before accepting the Faith. If, however, any act to the contrary be found, we command the princes and the potentate in their respective places that, under pain of excommunication, they shall cause the hereditary portion and property of these converts to be restored to them intact.[37]

The next pope, Innocent III, was likewise troubled by the economic situation of the new Christians, about which he wrote a great deal. In a letter of 5 December 1199 to the abbot and convent of Saint Mary de Pratt in Leicester, England, he writes that it had been brought to his attention that a Jew who had converted in the wake of the influence of a certain nobleman had descended to abject poverty. Innocent analyzes the problem with great clarity. He first emphasizes the theological importance of Jewish conversion to Christianity.

> The more the people afflicted by Jewish blindness attend to the superficial meaning of Divine Scriptures and fail to understand the quintessence of purity which these spiritual doctrines contain, the more it permits in its obduracy and permits itself, as up to now, to remain in the darkest shadow, so much the more ought we to rejoice in God because of those (of their number) who hold and embrace the true faith, and desire the propagation of the name of Christ.

Secondly, he warns that this theological success is likely to come to naught due to the (practical) difficulties confronted by the converts to Christianity:

> If thanks to the light of the Holy Spirit any have given up the errors of Judaism, and turning to that Light have accepted the Christian Faith, care must be taken that they should be solicitously provided for lest, in the midst of other faithful Christians, they become oppressed by lack of food. For, lacking the necessities of life, many of them, after their baptism, are led into great distress, with the result that they are often forced to go backward because of the avarice of such as are possessed of plenty, yet scorn to look at the Christian poor. Thus it is with our dear son R., the bearer of this letter. Despising rather than to wallow in the mire of wealth, he received the baptismal sacrament at the persuasion of a certain nobleman. But now that this man, who had supplied him with his necessities, went the way of all flesh, he is so weighted down with poverty that he has not the means by which to sustain his life.

Innocent III then makes clear to the abbot and the convent of Saint Mary de Pratt in Leicester what they need to do:

> Desiring that his wants should be supplied by you, we through Apostelic Letters, command Your Discretion, and we also warn you by your reverence for Him through whom this man received the light of truth, that you should provide him with his needs so that he may be suitably supplied with food and clothes. Know you this for certain, that we tolerate this situation with regret and with impatience, nor shall we be able to let this pass unnoticed if you should leave in any respect unaccomplished this command of ours, which in itself holds an act of piety. [38]

Like Alexander III at the Third Lateran Council, so too Innocent III wished to include this direction in the decision that had been taken in principle at the Fourth Lateran Council. The first decision stated that: 'Converts ought to be in better circumstances than they had been before accepting the Faith.'[39]

If one follows the papal involvement regarding the financing of converts to Christianity, one immediately sees that, throughout the thirteenth century, the popes needed to encourage representatives of the Church to assist these new Christians in their new life. The Magister family, which converted from the area of Mainz and Fulda, conducted an extensive correspondence with various popes over the course of twenty years until they received all that they had been promised prior to their conversion by Pope Innocent III. One need not add that the papal instructions were not always fulfilled, primarily by the higher and lower priesthood in various areas. Innocent III, Honorius III, and Gregory IX made every effort to ensure that the archbishops and bishops would transfer that which had been promised to the families of those who had converted. The head of a monastery in Hungary refused to finance two converts in 1235, and a large number of monasteries of men and women sought their privilege of exemption from financing and supporting converts to Christianity.[40] This tendency continued after the thirteenth century, and emerges clearly from the writings of Pope John XXII during the 1320s, in the wake of severe harm to the Jews. On the face of it, John XXII protects the Jews and advises the clergy not to force them to convert, but in the same breath strengthens the Christianity of those who had converted, even under duress, and emphasizes that one may not deprive them of their property. The reason given is that it would be absurd should people who enjoyed worldly goods and were prosperous when they were Jews become beggars once they convert to Christianity. This rule was fixed in canon law, where it continued throughout the fourteenth century.[41]

This change, whether or not it was implemented in practice, is clearly reflected in Jewish writings of the time. Grave doubts were already voiced at the beginning of the twelfth century over the tenth-century declaration by Rabbenu Gershom Meor ha-Golah regarding the inability of the apostate to inherit. R. Yitzhak ben Asher ha-Levi (d. 1133) turned his attention to the Talmud (*b. Bava Batra* 56a), which notes that Esau received his inheritance of Mount Seir from his father Isaac, who had received it as an inheritance from Abraham. That is, he found a source contradicting the argument brought by Rabbenu Gershom Meor ha-Golah stating that Esau received his inheritance outside of the inheritance of Abraham and Isaac. To the contrary, argues R. Yitzhak ben Asher ha-Levi, a section of Isaac's inheritance from Abraham was specifically given to Esau. Thus, R. Yitzhak ben Asher, at the beginning of the twelfth century, who sees Esau as symbolizing the Christian essence of the apostate, reaches the conclusion that 'the apostate inherits from his father.' But two generations later, at the end of the twelfth century, R. Eliezer ben Yoel ha-Levi establishes the principle that the children of the apostate are the heirs of his property and the apostate receives the inheritance of his father—albeit the Jewish court has the ability to prevent this. The work written by R. Eliezer ben Yoel ha-Levi, which portrays both situations—that in which the apostate inherits from his father, and that in which the son of the apostate inherits from his father—stemmed from the fact that R. Eliezer ben Yoel ha-Levi wished to validate the latter case, in which the children of a father who converted to Christianity inherit from him; but in order to do so he also had to validate the former case. It would appear that there were numerous such cases at the end of the twelfth century and the beginning of the thirteenth century, and R. Eliezer ben Yoel ha-Levi received a good number of such questions. He established the rule and strengthened the status of the Rabbinic Court as the final authority in every case. In one case, he was asked about a widow who had two daughters, one of whom had converted to Christianity but whose husband remained Jewish. Prior to her death the widow gave all of her property, as a deathbed gift (*matnat shekhiv mera*) to the daughter who remained Jewish, but the husband of the apostate daughter, who had himself remained Jewish, demanded his share of the inheritance.[42] In this case, R. Eliezer ben Yoel ha-Levi stated that, as when the father died she was still a Jew, the inheritance left by the mother also belonged to the daughter who had converted to Christianity, and through her to the husband.

But it would seem that the tendency that characterized earlier periods was to take over Jewish property which was left by the convert to Christianity and to pass it to those of his children or even grandchildren who had remained Jews. R. Yitzhak ben Moshe Or Zaru'a testifies, in the middle of the thirteenth century, that his teacher, Rabbi Simhah of Speyer, ruled that if the father is an apostate, his son who remains Jewish can inherit from his (Jewish) grandfather, thereby continuing the decision of Rashi stating that the relatives of the apostate are entitled to inherit from him. As proof, Rabbi Yitzhak ben Moshe brings a statement by Maimonides in his *Mishneh Torah*: 'A Jew who changed his religion inherits from his relatives as he would have [in the past], and if the Rabbinic Court saw fit to deprive him of his money and to impose a penalty upon him so that he not inherit, in order not to strengthen their [the apostates'] hand, they are allowed to do so. And if he has sons who are Jews, the inheritance of their apostate father is given to them; and this is the custom in the West [i.e., North Africa].'[43] In principle, this approach remained the regnant one in Germany, as we hear of similar decisions throughout the course of the fourteenth century. A case occurred during the fourteenth century that a certain person left money in the hands of another person; he thereafter died, and his son converted to Christianity. In principle, the deposit ought to have been returned to the apostate son, but the halakhic authorities responding to this question explicitly write that the one holding the deposit should not return it to the son, who is now a Christian, but rather hold it until such time as the son returns to Judaism; should this son die as a Christian, the Jewish relatives of the dead father will inherit his property.[44]

The change in the Christian position in support of those who convert to Christianity is echoed in the changing Jewish attitude, towards the end of the twelfth and throughout the course of the thirteenth century, to justify allowing converts to Christianity to recover their property. The Jewish tendency remains to attempt to preserve property within the Jewish framework and to give it to the close relatives of the convert, his children or even his grandchildren. Nevertheless, there was also a certain need to explain that, in that case where the rulers insist that the property remain in the hands of the converted Christian, this is not a fatal blow to the Jews' autonomous self-perception, which states that the Divine promise to Abraham and his seed leaves the situation of inheritance in Jewish hands alone. At this point, the Jews may attempt to preserve the property in their hands, but when they fail to do so it is justified through a theological perception that allows the 'new Esau' to inherit from his father Isaac.

Notes

1 Eliezer ben Nathan, *Sefer Even haEzer, Sefer Ra'avan*, Jerusalem 1984, *Bava Metzi'a* 85.

2 E. Kanarfogel, 'Returning to the Jewish Community in Medieval Ashkenaz: History and Halakhah,' *Turim*, Studies in Jewish History and Literature Presented to Dr. Bernard Lander, Vol. 1 ed. M. A. Shmidman, New York 2007, pp. 69–97.

3 See this question again in Chapter 5 concerning the status of convert women.

4 Tosafot *Pesahim* 92a s.v. *Aval*, s.v. *Tobel*.

5 Ya'akov ben Meir, *Sefer ha-Yashar* (News), ed. S. Schlesinger, Jerusalem 1959, No. 743, p. 434; Eliezer ben Samuel of Metz, *Sefer Yere'im*, Vilna 1901, No. 159.

6 Tosafot *Sanhedrin* 74b s.v. *vha Ester*. See the stand of Rabbenu Tam.

7 Isaac ben Moses, *Sefer Or Zarua*, 4 vols. Zhitomir 1862, Vol. 2, No. 428.

8 R. Chazan, 'The Blois Incident of 1171: A Study in Jewish Intercommunal

Organization,' *PAAJR (Proceedings of the American Academy for Jewish Research)* 36 (1968), pp. 13–31.

9 S. Goldin, 'Jewish Society under Pressure: The Concept of Childhood,' in: *Youth in the Middle Ages*, eds. P. J. Goldberg and F. Riddy, York 2004, pp. 29–43.

10 Tosafot *Pesahim* 92a s.v. *Aval*; Kanarfogel, 'Returning to the Jewish Community in Medieval Ashkenaz,' p. 76, note 16.

11 Kanarfogel, 'Returning to the Jewish Community in Medieval Ashkenaz,' pp. 69–97.

12 Zidkiya ben Abraham, *Sefer Shibolei haLeqet haShalem*, Vol. 2, Jerusalem 1969, pp. 180–190, No. 45; Shlomo ben Isaac (Rashi), *Sefer ha-Ora*, ed. S. Buber, Vol. 2, Lemberg 1905, No. 116, p. 216; Meir ben Baruch, *Sheelot u-Teshuvot ha-Maharam*, Prague edition, ed. M. A. Blakh, Budapest 1895, Nos. 791, 799; *Mordechai Bava Metzi'a*, No. 33.

13 E. E. Urbach, *The Tosaphists: Their History, Writings and Methods*, Jerusalem 1980, pp. 242–243, 244. Zidkiya ben Abraham, *Sefer Shibolei haLeqet*, Vol. 2, pp. 185–190, No. 46.

14 Zidkiya ben Abraham, *Sefer Shibolei haLeqet*, Vol. 2, pp. 185–190, No. 46,

15 Shlomo ben Isaac (Rashi), *Responsa Rashi*, No. 168. Most likely this answer is R'I's answer, so we can date it on the end of the thirteenth century. See Kanarfogel, 'Returning to the Jewish Community in Medieval Ashkenaz.'

16 Isaac ben Moses, *Sefer Or Zarua*, Vol. 1, No. 448; Moses of Zurich, *Sefer haSemak miZurich*, ed. I. J. Har-Shosanim, 3 vols. Jerusalem 1973, Vol. 2, No. 156, p. 48; Urbach, *The Tosaphists*, p. 265.

17 Shlomo ben Isaac (Rashi), *Responsa Rashi*, ed. I. Elfenbein, New York 1943, Nos. 173, 176; Shlomo ben Isaac (Rashi), *Sefer ha-Ora*, No. 99; Ya'akov ben Meir, *Sefer ha-Yashar* (News), No. 743; Meir ha-Kohen, *Teshuvot Maimuniut* to Moses ben Maimon, *Mishneh Tora*, Jerusalem 1952, *Mishpatim* No. 36; Tosafot *Avodah Zarah* 26b s.v. *Ani Shone*; Eliezer ben Samuel of Metz, *Sefer Yere'im*, No. 156; Isaac ben Moses, *Sefer Or Zarua*, Vol. 4, *Sanhedrin* No. 16; Moses of Coucy, *Semag: Sefer Mizvot Gadol*, Jerusalem 1961, *Ashin* No. 162; Meir ben Baruch, *Sheelot u-Teshuvot ha-Maharam*, Prague edition, Nos. 791, 799. Characteristic of this is the opinion of the Mordechai at the end of the thirteenth and beginning of the fourteenth centuries, see *Mordechai Avodah Zarah*, No. 814.

18 Isaac ben Moses, *Sefer Or Zarua*, Vol. 2, §112; *Teshuvot uPsakim, Responsa et Decisiones*, ed. E., Kupfer, Jerusalem 1973, No. 171, p. 290; Urbach, *The Tosaphists*, p. 417; Kanarfogel, 'Returning to the Jewish Community in Medieval Ashkenaz.'

19 Urbach, *The Tosaphists*, p. 407, about Moses of Zurich, *Sefer haSemak miZurich*, Vol. 2, No. 156, p. 48.

20 Tosafot *Megila* 13b; Isaac ben Moses, *Sefer Or Zarua*, Vol. 1, No. 112; they cite the story told in *Abot de-Rabbi Nathan*, as well as in the Talmudic tradition, relating to the immersion of Queen Esther every time she left the bedroom

where she had been with Ahasuerus. See Kanarfogel, 'Returning to the Jewish Community in Medieval Ashkenaz,' pp. 84–85 and note 16.

21 Isaac ben Moses, *Sefer Or Zarua*, Vol. 2, No. 428; Meir ben Baruch, *Sheelot u-Teshuvot ha-Maharam*, Prague edition, No. 544; *Mordechai Mo'ed Katan*, No. 886; Hayim ben Rabbi Yitzhak, *Responsa*, Leipzig 1860, No. 14; Urbach, *The Tosaphists*, p. 343; A. Grossman, *The Early Sages of Ashkenaz* [Hebrew], Jerusalem 1981, pp. 112–113.

22 *b. Mo'ed Katan* 25a; Rashi at *Shabbat* 105b.

23 *m. Sanhedrin* 4:5; *b. Sanhedrin* 39b.

24 A. Agus, ed., *Responsa of the Tosaphists*, New York 1954, No. 125.

25 I. Davidson, *Thesaurus of Medieval Hebrew Poetry* [Hebrew], 4 vols. New York 1970, Vol. 3, p. 409, No. 132.

26 A. David, 'Pogroms against French Jewry during the Shepherds' Crusade of 1251,' [Hebrew] *Tarbiz* 46 (1977), pp. 251–257.

27 Meir ha-Kohen, *Teshuvot Maimuniut* to Moses ben Maimon, *Mishneh Tora*, *Nashim* No. 10; *Haggahot Mordechai Ketubut*, No. 306.

28 Meir ben Baruch, *Sheelot u-Teshuvot ha-Maharam*, Prague edition, No. 544.

29 Isaac ben Moses, *Sefer Or Zarua*, Vol. 1, *Yibum* No. 605, p. 163.

30 Meir ben Baruch, *Sheelot u-Teshuvot ha-Maharam*, Prague edition, No. 1,022.

31 *Ketubah*—marriage contract by which a bridegroom obligates himself to provide a settlement for this wife if he divorces her, or through his heir if he predeceases her.

32 It is possible to date their responsum at the end of the thirteenth century, as the Rosh was still in Germany, and the Maharam of Rothenburg is referred to there as being deceased; hence the responsum must have been written between 1293 and 1300, and may reflect the period of violence against Jews in 1298, see: Agus, ed., *Responsa of the Tosaphists*, pp. 233–248, No. 128, pp. 235–247.

33 Quoting in this context *b. Sanhedrin* 74a and *Avodah Zarah* 27b.

34 Agus, *Responsa of the Tosaphists*, pp. 233–248, No. 128, pp. 235–247.

35 See above, Chapter 1.

36 From the privilege granted to the Jews of Vienna in 1238, repeated in 1360 by the archbishop of Cologne, and in France around 1381. S. Grayzel, *The Church and the Jews in the XIIIth Century*, rev. edition, New York 1966, pp. 18–19 (esp. note 36).

37 S. Simonsohn, *The Apostolic See and the Jews*, Toronto 1991, pp. 243–245; Grayzel, *The Church and the Jews in the XIIIth Century*, pp. 16–18, 296.

38 Simonsohn, *The Apostolic See and the Jews*, pp. 243–248; 'A new plant should be strengthened not alone by the dew of doctrine, but nourished also by temporal benefits'; Grayzel, *The Church and the Jews in the XIIIth Century*, p. 17 and No. 29, pp. 137–139.

39 Grayzel, *The Church and the Jews in the XIIIth Century*, pp. 136–138, No. 93.

40 Grayzel, *The Church and the Jews in the XIIIth Century*, pp. 164ff., Nos. 112, 140, 141, 146, 148, 161; Simonsohn, *The Apostolic See and the Jews*, pp. 247–248.

41 Simonsohn, *The Apostolic See and the Jews*, pp. 257–259.
42 Isaac ben Moses, *Sefer Or Zarua*, Vol. 3, *Bava Batra* No. 102; Meir ben Baruch, *Sheelot u-Teshuvot ha-Maharam*, Prague edition, No. 929.
43 Maimonides in his *Mishneh Torah*, *Hilkhot Nahalot* 6.12; Isaac ben Moses, *Sefer Or Zarua*, Vol. 3, *Bava Batra* Nos. 103–105; Meir ben Baruch, *Sheelot u-Teshuvot ha-Maharam*, Prague edition, No. 928; *Mordechai Kiddushin*, No. 492.
44 This responsum is signed by the leading rabbis of Mainz from the 1360s and 1370s; Hayim ben Rabbi Yitzhak, *Responsa*, No. 224.

5

Attitudes towards women

The Christian sources provide us with various examples of the fact that Jewish women voluntarily converted to Christianity and, moreover, that this female conversion was honest and authentic. As matters are presented by Miri Rubin: 'Women, like children, were more likely than men to become good converts as they were seen as pliant, easily influenced, and lacking in the adamant and obstinate preoccupation with Jewish law.'[1] The Christian sources speak primarily of Jewish women who were convinced of the truth of Christianity and converted to the Christian religion as the result of undergoing some miraculous experience. This point is particularly emphasized in those Christian sources describing attempts by Jews to profane the Host, the sacred bread, with depictions of Jewish women or girls (or even children) who participated against their will in attempts by their terrible fathers to harm the Host, and through it Jesus and the Christian world. When, for example, the Host is placed in a pot full of boiling water, the Jewish woman sees the image of a handsome, living child emerging from the boiling pot. She immediately understands that the divine truth is found on the Christian side rather than on the Jewish side, which is violent and tainted with sweat, and she immediately converts to Christianity. Women also discover the location of the Host which was stolen by Jews, and describe what the Jews do to profane the Host in order to cause harm to the Christian world.[2] From the 1270s on, we begin to hear of Jewish men and women in England who convert to Christianity as the result of the deliberate economic harm directed against them by the English lords in the days of Edward I, and the promise given Jews to finance their life in the Domus Conversorum ('Jewish house'). As a result, one finds in legal documents and in reports made to the king information concerning these houses, including numerous details relating to Jews and Jewesses who convert in order to seek financial help and assistance among the Christians, who offer them a false hope of protected Christian life.[3] It is possible to learn much from these historical sources regarding Jewish women who convert to Christianity.

The first and most striking characteristic of Jewish writing about women and the question of their conversion is that the literature describes very few women who converted to Christianity of their own free will. As we have seen, the responsa literature relates to cases in which the husband converted to Christianity and his wife insisted on remaining Jewish, despite the new and problematic situation thereby created for her. In the Jewish literature of martyrdom, written by men, women who killed themselves as martyrs for Kiddush Hashem during the First Crusades are a key motif. And indeed, the chronicles reveal that women died as martyrs in almost as great numbers as did men.[4] Generally speaking, when we read in Jewish writings about women who converted out, the testimonies almost always concern women who were kidnapped by Christians and held against their will, and usually succeeded in freeing themselves from the Christian captivity, whether as a result of bribery or as a result of being released by the Christians.

The halakhic background here is the need to make decisions regarding what to do with such women. As in many other situations, the halakhic authorities attempted a decision on the basis of precedent through use of an earlier, similar discussion in the Talmud. The Mishnah and the Talmud contain discussions clarifying the circumstances under which a woman who has been held captive may return to her husband (after her husband, who is obligated to redeem her from captivity, in fact did so). The discussions there revolve in practice around the question of the nature of the captors. If the captors took women in order to hold them for ransom, it is clear that they would have been protected from assault, in which case the woman may return to her husband. But if the captors were interested in murdering and despoiling, then it is suspected that the woman may have offered herself to them in order to remain alive. In that case, the issue at hand is whether or not she can return to her husband after her release from captivity. During this period of captivity, one who was forced to convert was presumed to be a captive of the first kind; hence, most of the Sages conclude that she is allowed to return to her husband.[5] Moreover, a number of the Rabbis even state that one may not necessarily draw inferences from the case brought in the Mishnah and discussed in the Talmud to their own time, as the Christians who seize women in order to convert them to Christianity wished to convince them to convert to the rival religion; hence, it would make no sense for them to behave towards them in a problematic or licentious way. In other words, the medieval cases correspond neither to the latter nor to the former case.

In order to understand this phenomenon, one needs to analyze extensively a particular case described in some detail in both the Jewish and Christian sources.[6] On 24 May 1241, the Jewish community of Frankfurt-on-Main was attacked with disastrous results. In the Jewish sources, the case is described as a particularly violent attack by Christians against a peaceful and believing Jewish community in an attempt to forcibly impose upon them conversion to Christianity. The German chronicle, by contrast, emphasizes that the upheaval was the result of an attempt by the Jewish community to prevent one of the members of the community from converting to Christianity. As a result—and due to the behavior of the Jews—we are told by the German chronicle that 'several Christians' were harmed, and some 180 Jews were killed by the sword or by fire.[7] In a fire which was set by the Jews, the buildings of the communities and almost half the town burned down. Twenty-four Jews, who did not die by fire or sword, converted to Christianity.

> The son of a Jew in the royal city of Frankfurt wished to receive the baptism of the Christian faith and was prevented from doing so by his relatives and friends. Therefore a public dispute ensued between Christians and Jews ... they fought very violently between them. A few Christians were killed thereby, while among the Jews 180 were, by sword and by fire which they had set in their own homes. Then the fire spread and burned nearly half the city. Perceiving imminent death, 24 Jews, who were neither slayed nor burned, let themselves be baptized.'[8]

Among those forcibly converted was a young woman, whose name unfortunately is not mentioned, who was engaged to a man from Würzburg named Yaakov ben Yoel. She was captured and held by the Christians for a month or two, but succeeded in returning to Jewishness, and to Würzburg in order to find her fiancé and marry him. There it became clear to her that, in the interim, her intended had married another woman. The case came before the Jewish court, where there ensued a lively debate among the judges who presented a variety of opinions portraying the attitude of the leadership towards this subject.[9]

Rabbi Yitzhak ben Moshe, who was the leading authority in Würzburg, retroactively approved the validity of the young man's marriage. True, he argued that he had counseled the family of the groom to wait until his fiancée could be freed and only then take counsel with the leadership as to whether he could marry another woman but, as the young man had

married despite this advice, the marriage was retroactively considered to
be valid. At this point, the young woman appealed to the court (evidently)
demanding that Yaakov of Würzburg divorce his wife and marry his former
fiancée. According to R. Yitzhak this was impossible; because she had been
held in captivity among Christians, his halakhic conclusion was that she was
unable to marry the boy.

R. Yitzhak ben Moshe's opinion had a double basis. First, he relied upon
the Talmudic discussion mentioned earlier in order to reach a decisive
conclusion: as the captors endangered the woman's life, one may assume
that she offered herself to them and therefore cannot continue in the
process of marriage to her intended bridegroom. Secondly, he works on
the assumption that a woman in a situation of danger and who escaped
may be presumed to have used her body in order to save herself. Here
R. Yitzhak ben Moshe relied upon the statement in *b. Avodah Zarah* 25b,
'A woman has her weapon upon her'—meaning, a woman need not fear
murder by Gentiles because she is able to save herself through the use of
her body. Indeed, in his eyes the fact that she managed to flee strengthened
the presumption that she used her body in order to survive. R. Yitzhak
ben Moshe concludes, therefore, that if she had been a married woman he
would have ruled that she could not return to her husband. Hence, as an
engaged woman she is similarly not permitted to return to her fiancé, and
his marriage to another woman is legitimate.

Behind the halakhic validity, there emerges from the writings of
R. Yitzhak ben Moshe a certain perception of the Christian religion as a
corrupt and immoral one, contaminated and dangerous. Hence he admires
those who died for Kiddush Hashem and refused to accept Christianity, even
for appearances. He particularly celebrates those women who preferred to
commit suicide for Kiddush Hashem rather than to convert to Christianity
under any condition, defining the Christians as immersed in carnal desires
and despising those Jewish women who were forcibly converted; he suspects
the Christians of violating such women even before their conversion to
Christianity. He contrasts those women who converted to Christianity with
those who died for Kiddush Hashem: 'For this our hearts grieve, and it is
fitting to be pained and to mourn for the righteous ones who were killed in
Frankfurt. Happy are they and happy is their portion, that they sanctified
with their bodies the honorable and awesome Name, and it is good for their
souls, for they caused good to themselves.'[10] The expressions, 'sanctified
with their bodies' and 'good to their souls' indicate, more than anything
else, what his opinion was of those who did not sanctify the Name with
their bodies and did not do good to their souls. Hence, he sees a woman

who was baptized to Christianity, even against her will, as one who had been free with her body, and finds Talmudic legitimacy for not requiring the man to return to his fiancée.

R. Yehudah ben Moshe ha-Cohen of Freiburg vociferously opposed the behavior of the young man and the ruling of R. Yitzhak ben Moshe. He sent letters 'to every city,' calling on them to defend this young woman in particular, and all those Jewish girls who had fallen victim to Christian coercion. His call is answered by other leaders, who in turn sent out their own letters: R. Yehudah ben Moshe ha-Cohen, R. Meshullam ben David, R. David ben Shealtiel, R. Shmuel ben Avraham of Speyer.[11]

These authors represent a different perception from that of R. Yitzhak ben Moshe regarding the attitude towards women who had been forced to convert. They do not deny the effort made by Christians to convert Jews, and perhaps in particular Jewish women, but they are also aware of the fact that in their day the Christian struggle had assumed a new face. The Christians are (primarily) interested in persuading women to convert to Christianity as a sign of its clear victory over Judaism; hence they intensify their efforts at convincing Jews. Even if the women were initially held forcibly by the Christians, their main intent would be to persuade them to remain Christians. Hence, in the opinion of these rabbis, as Christianity at this time was interested primarily in victory over Judaism, and the Christians made efforts to influence those girls whom they forcibly held to voluntarily convert to Christianity, from the moment these girls underwent forced baptism they were protected from sexual assault and were not subject to the threats of either physical attack or danger to life. It would be inconceivable that these young women would be raped by their Christian captors, just as it was inconceivable to suspect them of offering their favors in order to escape from death. These rabbis thus represent an approach that sees the women who were held by the Christians specifically as a sterling example of those who were unwilling to forego their Judaism. From an halakhic viewpoint they reject the Talmudic model which sees them as 'captive' or 'held in mortal danger' (*shevuyah*; *nehbeshet la-nefashot*). In their opinion, they are in a third state: that of a woman who knows that she has been unlawfully captured, has not given up hope of being freed, and hence does not lose hope but constantly longs to return to her family and to her Jewishness.

Rabbi Meshullam ben David cites the rule established by his teacher, R. Simhah of Speyer: that if the women captured by the Christians think that it is possible for them to be freed by means of pressure on their captors or by bribery, and do not consider remaining Christians, they are deserving of and entitled to return to their husbands. This view

turns the Mishnaic discussion on its head, because these women are not
threatened in a physical manner, are not subject to sexual coercion, and
have not given up on returning to Jewishness. The case of the young
woman discussed here, specifically, is exemplary: she remains loyal to
Jewishness, denies Christianity even though it was imposed upon her to
convert to Christianity, and refuses to be married to an important and
wealthy Christian. Her answer is: 'I do not want him, because I am engaged
to a Hebrew.' The Christians, reporting the events in all innocence, stated
that she and others maintained their integrity and their Jewishness as far as
possible.[12] Moreover, it seems clear that these women were waiting every
day to be freed from the Christians who were holding them. The fact that,
in the final event, they did succeed in escaping from the Christians is taken
as indication that God responded to their deserving behavior and saved
them in a miraculous way. By contrast, the man—her erstwhile fiancé—
behaved in the worst imaginable way in that he violated his engagement
agreement, an act tantamount in their opinion to violating the *Herem* of
Rabbenu Gershom.[13] R. Meshullam's words are directed primarily against
R. Yitzhak ben Moshe: that one must protect these women, specifically
in light of the new Christian tactic of holding them forcibly and trying to
persuade them to convert to Christianity. It follows from this, not only
that they ought not to be punished for failing to die for Kiddush Hashem,
but that their behavior is particularly praiseworthy because they attempted
to free themselves from the clutches of Christianity in whatever way
possible. Moreover, the behavior of the faithless man is likely to weaken
those women who find themselves in similar situations in the future.
R. Meshullam emphasizes here the existence of a precedent for the present
case where, because of concern regarding the *Herem* of Rabbenu Gershom
Meor ha-Golah, the man was forced to divorce the woman he had married
and to marry the one whom he had originally promised.

   R. Yehudah ben Moshe ha-Cohen's words are primarily intended to
strengthen the Jewish self-image. The Jewish women are pure, and the
Christian captivity does not touch them. His words are formulated carefully:
the women were persuaded (to convert) with the threat of the sword, but
throughout the entire time their hearts were directed to their Heavenly
Father. He refers to them with the term, *banot mehutavot,* 'daughters like
corner pillars.' This term is one of great significance, based upon associ-
ations with a verse in Psalms describing a man's sons and daughters: 'May
our sons in their youth be like plants, full grown; our daughters like corner
pillars, cut for the structure of a palace' (Psalms 144:12). Since the eleventh
century, the widely accepted interpretation of the phrase 'our daughters

like corner pillars, cut for the structure of the palace' is that it describes the appropriate manner of behavior of Jewish women concerning purity in matters of intimate relations. Rashi, in his commentary on the Talmud, explains the term by noting that it combines the reference to 'olives' in the above-mentioned verse from Psalms with the 'olives' mentioned in Zechariah 9:15: 'drenched like the corners of the altar.' The 'sprinklers' in the Sanctuary and in the Temple were vessels used for sprinkling blood upon the altar. In Rashi's view, the sprinkler filled with the blood of the sacrifice is compared to a married woman, filled with desire and awaiting her husband alone, and keeping herself for her husband, be things as they may. According to his view, such women are the foundation upon which there stand the walls of the Sanctuary, the walls of the Temple and, by extension, the entire structure of the Jewish people. That is to say, R. Yehudah emphasizes the standing of pure, upright Jewish women as the walls (or pillars) of the Sanctuary.[14]

R. Yehudah ben Moshe ha-Cohen and R. Shmuel ben Avraham, both of whom were among those who attacked the ruling of R. Yitzhak ben Moshe, each composed a memorial poem concerning the event that had taken place in Frankfurt. These liturgical poems were intended to be recited on the anniversary days of the slaughter, while mentioning the names of those who died 'sanctifying the Name.' These *piyyutim* describe the willingness to die, the attachment to the Jewish faith, and the attempt by the Christians to impose their religion by force and thereby achieve victory. The list evidently names those who died out of active opposition to Christian coercion, while the others were put to death by the sword or burnt to death in a fire that broke out.[15] This was unlike the writings of R. Yitzhak ben Moshe, who contrasts those women who were forcibly converted to Christianity and remained alive against the noble behavior of those who did not agree to convert and died a glorious death. These two authors do not emphasize this element at all. Their *piyyutim* describe the Jewish community as a single group, its members having identical behavior, both men and women. R. Yehudah ben Moshe goes even further: in his poem, he describes the women who died for Kiddush Hashem as 'corner-pillar daughters,' the same term used in his responsum to refer to those women who were forced to live as Christians and returned to Judaism with all their heart. In this *piyyut*, he expresses his view that, in practice, there is no difference between those women who died for Kiddush Hashem and those who were forcibly converted to Christianity but continued to observe Judaism. Both groups are certainly pure from the sexual viewpoint: some of them chose to die for Kiddush Hashem, while others were forced to convert but even then preserved their purity and their faith. Likewise R. Shmuel ben Avraham, in the *piyyut* which he wrote, glorifies the men and women who die for Kiddush Hashem, but in his responsum attacks the distinction drawn by R. Yitzhak ben Moshe regarding those women who were forced to live as Christians and then returned to their Judaism by using identical terms for both. As against the halakhic argument invoked by R. Yitzhak, R. Shmuel writes quite simply, in a brief sentence, 'I do not know who allowed him to see daughters of Israel as presumed to be harlots.'[16]

Another respondent, R. David ben Shealtiel, criticized primarily the halakhic viewpoint of R. Yitzhak Or Zaru'a. He reiterated what Rabbenu Hannanel had already explained, that the precedents brought in the Talmud relate, in their own time (i.e., the Middle Ages), only to those women married to *kohanim* (members of the hereditary 'priesthood'), thereby greatly limiting the applicability of such precedents. As for the fact that the woman had spent a certain period of time living among Christians as a Christian woman, R. David ben Shealtiel emphasized the view articulated in the Talmud by the *amora* Ravva: 'If it [i.e., her relations with a gentile man] began through coercion, [even] if was subsequently done willingly, she is permitted (to her husband).' In the present case, it clearly began with coercion, and also continued under duress. He adds that it is well known that in France Rabbenu Tam allowed the return of women to their husbands after they had spent a period of time among Christians. Finally, he cites the opinion of R. Eliezer ben Yoel ha-Levi (Rabya'h; beginning of the thirteenth century) stating that, wherever there are Christian judges in the city, one may not assume that Christians violate Jewish women being held by them, and therefore one may not assume that the Christians violated them sexually. As for the young man who hastened to marry another woman despite the fact that he was already engaged to the former, R. David ben Shealtiel states that:

> This one who was unfaithful to his fiancée is deserving to be stretched upon the post and made to pay a serious fine, and I decree upon him under sanction of ban and excommunication to return to his fiancée; and if he has married the second one he must divorce her under the order of the community, and if he refuses he shall be subject to the ban and excommunication of the community; and if he adds to his previous sin the crime of marrying or betrothing the second one, let him incline his ear to the words of the Sages.[17]

It should be noted that, notwithstanding the strident opinion expressed in this case against the young man and on behalf of the young woman, the view that women ought to sacrifice their lives and refuse to agree to conversion even at the cost of their lives continued to be the predominant view of many of the men. This is clearly expressed by R. Asher ben Yehiel (Rosh) at the end of the thirteenth century. Despite the fact that, in his opinion, these women are permitted to return to their husbands, he judges them strictly in terms of values, referring to them as 'women who did not have the strength to stand in the palace of the king.' This is a clear allusion to Daniel 1:4: 'youths without blemish, handsome and skillful in all wisdom, endowed with knowledge, understanding learning, and competent to serve in the king's palace, and to teach them the letters and language of the Chaldeans.' Those able 'to serve in the king's palace' are those who are prepared to sacrifice themselves for their faith. According to the Rosh, these women must regret that they converted their religion, even under duress, even more so than those women who voluntarily converted to the Christian religion, for specifically in the case of forcible attempts to change one's religion one must be stubborn and die a martyr's death.[18]

The problematic case reflects a state in which a woman who was taken captive by Christians refused to become integrated within the Christian world in which she was forced to live and, despite the temptations offered by Christian society, insisted upon returning to her Jewishness. But what if the woman forced to live within the Christian world feels so good about it that she does not hasten to return to the Jewish world? Such a case was in fact brought to our attention regarding a woman who was captured by Christians and forcibly converted to Christianity, who went on to live in marriage with a Christian man. After a certain period of time, her parents succeeded in bringing her back, and she returned to living with her Jewish husband. It becomes clear that, in practice, the woman has returned to her husband, and the society around her accepts this. However, one member of the community was troubled by this situation and sent an inquiry about it to the Rabbinic judges: this woman had lived with a Gentile for a certain period of time; how then can she return to her Jewish husband? 'And I asked them: Who permitted her to her husband [because a woman who has been unfaithful to her husband is forbidden to him thereafter]? ... And now, our Rabbis, teach us the way in which we should walk, for I do not know how to rule in this matter!' The question is, in practice, how to relate to this woman in light of the Talmudic precedents.[19]

The case here involved a woman who had been forced to convert under threat to her life, but who did not give herself over to death for Kiddush Hashem, subsequently remained in Christianity of her own free will, lived intimately with a Christian man, and 'behaved licentiously regarding all the prohibitions of the Torah.' Is such a woman comparable to one who abandoned her husband and now lives with another man, in which case she is clearly forbidden to return to her husband? Or shall we treat such a woman on the basis of her 'beginning'—i.e., as one who was taken captive unwillingly, and conclude that she deserves to return to her husband? The degree to which this matter was problematic may be seen on the basis of the answer, which may be understood in both directions: the author of the responsum is concerned that, if we permit a situation in which a woman who had voluntarily lived with a Christian man returns to Judaism and lives with her Jewish husband as before, merely because she had originally been taken captive forcibly by the Christians, this will be the beginning of a 'slippery slope' ('we will destroy the entire structure'). This is particularly so in light of the fact that she did not attempt to escape or slip away from the Christians immediately. However, at the end of his words he withdraws somewhat from his uncompromising position and returns the question to his interlocutor: 'I have not heard the halakhah regarding this subject from my rabbis, and you are wise like an angel of God.'[20]

This case, like several others, reveals what the sources wished to obscure (if not to conceal entirely): namely, that there were Jewish women who converted to Christianity of their own free will and lived with Christian men. We become aware of such cases only when the women wish to return to their Jewishness, or even wish to return to their Jewishness together with the Christian man with whom they live who is now interested in conversion to Judaism, in which case the reality becomes evident in the course of the halakhic discussion.

The earliest source concerning this matter is a responsum attributed to Rashi (end of the eleventh century, northern France), concerning a married woman who lives willingly with a Christian man, and is now interested in returning to live with her husband. Is she permitted to him or not?[21] This responsum is extremely interesting, over and above the brief and clear statement that a married woman who converted to Christianity and lived with a Gentile is forbidden to her Jewish husband—first of all, in the use which it makes of the case of Queen Esther in order to prove this point (a subject to be discussed in the next example); secondly, in the assumption that a woman converts to Christianity because of her desire to live with a Christian man, and not because she is convinced of the truth of the Christian religion. It does not seem possible to our author that a woman would be convinced of the Christian truth; hence, her reason for abandoning the Jewish religion must be her desire to indulge in sexual relations which are forbidden by the Jewish religion but permitted according to Christianity. This substantive position, one of a positive and value-based self-definition as opposed to the other religion, is based upon a passage in the Talmud: 'R. Yehudah said in the name of Rav: Israel knew that idolatry has no substance; hence, they did not engage in pagan worship except to permit themselves sexual licentiousness in public' (*b. Sanhedrin* 63b). Thus, a woman who converted to Christianity is perceived as one who had surrendered to her sexual lust.[22] At the end of the responsum, its author takes care to note that there are those who think differently, whom he refers to as 'chatterers': 'There are those who chatter regarding this matter, and there is naught of substance to their words... and one may not be lenient.'[23] That is, the decisive response that 'one may not be lenient,' and the reference to those who differ as 'chatterers,' indicates a different attitude towards these women. A debate of this type takes place between the grandson of Rashi, R. Ya'akov ben Meir Tam, and his disciple, R. Yaakov ben Mordechai, regarding an interesting case in which a woman converts to Christianity voluntarily, lives with a Christian, and now wishes to return to Judaism, along with the Christian man, who is interested in converting. Such a case was brought before Rabbenu Tam (d. 1171), who states that she may return and is even permitted to marry the same Christian once he converts.[24]

Rabbi Ya'akov Tam's remarks relate to a discussion in the Talmud regarding the question as to whether a woman threatened with rape by non-Jews needs to resist to the point of death (i.e., effectively, to commit suicide). Or, to be more precise, is one required to inform women that the case of sexual violation by a Gentile does not disqualify her from returning to her husband, and is not a cause for sacrificing her life? This discussion refers in practice to *jus primae noctis*, mentioned in the Talmud with respect to the Hasmonean or Roman period; the answer given in the Talmud is that one ought not to publicize this fact, as there may be women who would consent willingly, and hence would not be allowed to return to their husbands.[25] The question asked in the Middle Ages concerning this matter was whether the principle that one is required to sacrifice one's life in three cases (idolatry, sexual licentiousness, and bloodshed) also subsumes the case of rape by a Gentile.

Rabbenu Tam states, in all simplicity, that the sexual intercourse of somebody who is not a Jew is not considered *giluy arayot*, a forbidden sexual act, because their coitus cannot be described as such because they are compared to animals. His argument for this is based upon Ezekiel 23:20: 'and their issue is like that of horses,' a verse referring to Gentiles. He cites in proof the case of Queen Esther. The Talmud asks the question why, regarding Esther she did not sacrifice her life, despite the fact that her act of cohabiting with the Gentile King Ahasuerus was one that was publicly known, and as such an act for which one is required to sacrifice one's life (*b. Sanhedrin* 74a). Because the question is raised regarding the public nature of the act and not regarding it being a prohibited sexual act, Rabbenu Tam infers that the Talmud assumes that in the case of Esther there was no *giluy arayot*, because the intercourse of the Gentiles is not considered as such at all, because they are like animals. This conclusion eliminates the problem entirely. If the sexual act of a person who is not Jewish is not considered as a human act, then there is no reason to apply the rule that one who was unfaithful to her husband is prohibited to both her husband and her lover; there is likewise no problem involved regarding a woman who was raped by a Gentile; and there is also no problem for a Jewish woman who lived with a Gentile man to return to Judaism and also to marry the same man after he converts.

This approach of Rabbenu Tam is unacceptable to Rabbi Yaakov ben Mordechai. As he understands matters, the decisive factor is the will of the woman, and if the woman voluntarily agreed to intercourse she is prohibited to her husband. He also brings proof (among other things) from the case of Queen Esther. According to the medieval explanation, Esther was Mordechai's wife before she came into Ahasuerus' harem, and she continued her relations with Mordechai until she set out to seduce Ahasuerus of her own intiative, at which point she said, 'If I perish, I perish' (Esther 4:16)—that is to say, from this moment on she was giving herself to Ahasuerus of her own free will; hence, from that point she was considered unfaithful to Mordechai and therefore forbidden to him, despite the fact that Ahasuerus was not a Jew. We conclude from this that adultery with a Gentile renders a woman forbidden to her husband, and that his intercourse is not treated as analogous to that of an animal.

Another woman discussed in this context is Yael, wife of Heber the Kenite (*b. Sanhedrin* 105b), concerning whom it is said, 'Most blessed of women in the tent is Yael' (Judges 5:24). Regarding the question, to which women is she is compared here, the Talmud answers, 'Sarah, Rebecca, Rachel and Leah' (*b. Nazir* 23a). But how is it that Yael is considered so blessed? Did she not have forbidden sexual relations with Sisera? Yael was not raped, as Sisera did not force himself upon her; to the contrary, he was completely dependent upon her and tried to hide himself with her in order to save himself from Barak who was chasing him. The explanation given is that Yael's act—i.e., the transgression involved in having sexual relations with Sisera—was done in order to kill him and thereby save Israel, indicating that 'A transgression for its own sake is greater than a mitzvah for its own sake.'[26] That is, Yael performed a transgression in order to save her people; hence, she is even more highly praised than the mothers of the nation!

But at the end of the thirteenth century it is emphasized that one who converted of her own free will and lived with a Christian is forbidden to her husband if she returns to Judaism; as everything depends upon the woman's will, it is assumed that, when she converted to Christianity, she did so, not because she found Christianity attractive as a religion, but because she wanted to be unfaithful to her husband. In this manner, the argument that the woman converted because she recognized Christianity as the true religion is rejected. But from the sources the prevalent reality becomes clear: husbands were willing to accept their wives back when they returned from the Christian world, even when they knew that this was contrary to the halakhah and that the religious leadership and the judges were opposed to this. Rashi himself stated that such a woman must receive a divorce from her husband. Some hundred years later, R. Eliezer ben Yoel ha-Levi testified that his father permitted a married woman who had willingly spent a certain period of time in the home of a Christian man to return to her husband. But particularly, the understanding that the woman is forbidden to her husband is shown by the explicit anger of R. Isaiah di Trani in the middle of the thirteenth century regarding such a situation: 'I have heard of a great ill that is done in your community that a married woman who had become an apostate and stayed among the Gentiles many days thereafter returned and resumed relations with her husband as it was before.' This also applies to the previous case which, it is true, concerns a woman who was forcibly taken captive by the Gentiles, but thereafter remained with them of her own free will and lived with a Gentile, who now returned and lived with the man who had previously been her husband.[27]

At the beginning of the thirteenth century, Rabbi Yitzhak of Nicola (apparently Lincoln) writes of 'a woman who willingly had illicit relations with a Gentile and became an apostate, and thereafter recanted [returned to Judaism] and went to a remote country, whose mother complained that her son-in-law [had since] married another woman but would not agree to divorce her daughter [the first wife], who had since repented.'[28] In other words, there existed a phenomenon of Jewish women who lived with Christian men. Moreover, generally speaking the husbands were willing to accept them back as their wives once they returned to the bosom of Judaism.

The tension between halakhah and reality also emerges regarding the question as to what happens if both partners converted together to

Christianity, and now wish to return to Judaism and continue to live as husband and wife. This question was raised at the end of the twelfth century in northern France, and again a century later in Germany. Rabbi Samson of Sens (d. 1230) responded with much reservation regarding such a case brought to his attention, in which one of the Sages stated that the woman is presumed to have been sexually loose, even though her husband was with her, and therefore is forbidden to him following his return to Judaism. R. Samson emphasizes that, even among non-Jews, women are not usually sexually licentious, and therefore it seems unreasonable to assume that a Jewish woman who lived among Christians would be of a lower moral level than the Christians themselves. Moreover, he stresses the fact that both of them were 'repentants' and wished to return to Judaism—a fact which indicates that, in his opinion, they did not violate Torah prohibitions during the period when they were Christians. It is clear that the essence of his decision is the desire to allow them to return to Judaism, and is clear that they wish to return to Judaism in order to live together as a Jewish couple. It they were to be separated, perhaps this would prevent them from returning to Judaism.

In Germany, at the end of the thirteenth or the beginning of the fourteenth century, the debate on this matter revolves around the salient halakhic points regarding this subject. However, the attitude of anger towards the apostates, particularly towards the women who had converted, is strongly emphasized. We are dealing here with a couple who had abandoned Judaism and chosen to live among Christians, and it is possible that the sexual 'freedom,' specifically, may have been what attracted them. This is particularly true, in the leadership's opinion, with regard to the woman. One may not rely upon a woman who has converted to Christianity to maintain her chastity for her husband, for 'If she does not fear the Holy One blessed be He, why should she fear her husband?' Nevertheless, the reality is reflected in their decision. Notwithstanding these views, such couples return together to Judaism and once again live together as Jews. It seems clear that the leadership was unable and unwilling to separate them. In the words of one of the authors of the response: 'So as not to reject them so that they return to their bad ways, I saw fit that one ought not to be strict with them.'[29]

Rabbi Meir ben Baruch (the Maharam of Rothenburg) who, as we have seen, was very strict in his approach towards men who had converted to Christianity and now wished to returned to Judaism, was much more lenient with women in Dukenhausen (Rockenhausen?) who found themselves in a similar situation. He accepted the testimony of the women themselves, as well as permitting them to return to their husbands. He emphasizes that 'they never practiced idolatry, but the priest said his abomination to the Gentiles and they remained silent.'[30] This is the dominant approach in the halakhic rulings of the end of the thirteenth and beginning of the fourteenth centuries. All of these Sages see a married woman who was captured by Christians and thereafter released as one who should be allowed to return to her husband without difficulty; in the case of divorce, she is entitled to the full sum of her *ketubah*. As we observed earlier, they were also willing to distinguish what happened in their own period from the seeming precedent from the Talmud. The Christians are interested in these women as potential Christians; hence, they will protect them and will not assault them sexually. The rabbis emphasize that these women were forced to convert under coercion and that 'it is their constant intention to return to Judaism'—that is to say, they have not given up hope on the possibility of returning to Judaism, and even endangered themselves by their attempts to return. One may therefore accept their testimony regarding one another, even from the period during which they were 'Christians' under coercion.[31]

Was the approach here one that was built upon reality? Did women convert to Christianity less often than men? As we do not have any evidence one way or another, I would like to emphasize a point related to their self-definition as Jews and to the mentality in relation to women. The Jews in the Middle Ages believed that conversion to Christianity, even under force and even for a brief period of time, created a substantive blemish in the personality of the convert and in the transmission of their qualities. As I understand the matter, medieval Jewish society believed that women were responsible for transmitting the 'genetic' qualities of Jewishness to their children; hence, there was a constant worry about the situation of women and the dangers involved in their being drawn close to Christianity. The insistence upon searching out family 'blemishes' was directed primarily towards future brides, particularly if they belonged to families in which there had been apostates or forced converts to Christianity.[32] In the mid-twelfth century, in northern France, Rabbenu Tam received a letter stating that in a certain family there was a daughter who had been married to a man who converted to Christianity and that she had received a divorce from him; however, one of the judges refused to ratify the *get* and it was now difficult for the woman to remarry. Rabbenu Tam answers that, if there is a divorce written by an apostate, the woman may marry whomever she wishes, adding that, 'Now you, the generous father of the daughter, marry your daughter to one who is fitting to her, for there is no need to pay any attention to the words of scandal-mongers.'[33]

In other words: society was fearful of any connection with a person who had been touched in whatever way by the Christian religion. One hundred years later, in Germany, there was a case involving a family whose son was engaged to a girl who had fallen into the captivity of Christians, so they quickly married him to someone else. They evidently feared that, as the girl had been in Christian hands, she was contaminated in some way and, as the fiancée of their son, he would have to marry her should she be released, and the blemish would enter into their family. The rabbis sought to mollify fears regarding such women and were therefore insistent upon emphasizing the role of women in martyrology, on the one hand, and moderating the attitude towards women who had been forced to convert but had returned to Judaism, on the other.

Notes

1 M. Rubin, *Gentile Tales: The Narrative Assault on Late Medieval Jews*, London 1999, p. 84.

2 See Rudolph of Schlettstadt story—*Historiae memorables. Zur Dominikanerliteratur und Kulturgeschichte des 13 Jahrhunderts*, ed. E. Kleinschnidt, Cologne 1974, No. 9, pp. 53–55; R. Po-chia Hsia, 'Witchcraft, Magic and the Jews in Late Medieval and Early Modern Germany,' in: *From Witness to Witchcraft: Jews and Judaism in Medieval Christian Thought*, ed. J. Cohen, Wiesbaden 1997, pp. 419–433; Rubin, *Gentile Tales*, pp. 84–86.

3 M. Adler, *Jews of Medieval England,* London 1939, pp. 279–339; R. C. Stacey, 'The Conversion of Jews to Christianity in Thirteenth-Century England,' *Speculum* 67 (1992), pp. 263–283; R. Mundill, *England's Jewish Solution*, Cambridge 1998, pp. 100–103, 275–276.

4 S. Salfeld, *Das Martyrlogium des Nürnberger Memorbuches*, Berlin 1938; S. Noble, 'The Jewish Woman in Medieval Martyrology,' *Studies in Jewish Bibliography, History and Literature in honor of I. E. Kiev*, ed. C. Berlin, New York 1971, pp. 347–355. See also this article in: *Proceedings of the Fifth World Congress of the Jewish Studies*, 2 (1972), pp. 133–140; S. Goldin, *The Ways of Jewish Martyrdom*, Turnhout 2008, pp. 112–117.

5 *b. Ketubot* 26b Rashi and Tosafot there, Tosafot *Avodah Zarah* 23a s.v. *teda*; Rashi, *Avodah Zarah* 25b s.v. *Beisah*; Tosafot there s.v. *ica benyehu; Haggahot Maimuniyyot* to *Hilkhot Biaha* 18a; Meir ben Baruch, *Sheelot u-Teshuvot ha-Maharam*, Prague edition, ed. M. A. Blakh, Budapest 1895, No. 1,020; G. J. Blidstein, 'The Personal Status of Apostate and Ransomed Women in Medieval Jewish Law,' [Hebrew] *Shenaton ha-Mishpat ha-Ivri* 3–4 (1976–77), pp. 35–116.

6 S. W. Baron, *A Social and Religious History of the Jews*, 18 vols. Philadelphia 1952–83, Vol. 9, pp. 143–144; Blidstein, 'The Personal Status of Apostate,' note 200; Goldin, *The Ways of Jewish Martyrdom*, pp. 304–310; R. Furst,

'Captivity, Conversion and Communal Identity: Sexual Angst and Religious Crisis in Frankfurt, 1241,' *Jewish History* 2 (2008), pp. 179–221.

7 Names of the Dead: S. Salfeld, *Das Martyrlogium des Nürnberger Memorbuches*, Berlin 1938, pp. 13–14; 125–126.

8 *Monumenta Germaniae Historica – Scriptorium*, Vol. 16, pp. 26–40, the English translation from Frust, 'Captivity, Conversion, and Communal Identity,' p. 181.

9 The Responsa: *Responsa et Decisiones*, ed. E. Kupfer, Jerusalem 1973, pp. 282–289. Hayim ben Rabbi Yitzhak, *Responsa*, Leipzig 1860, No. 221; *Mordechai Ketubot*, No. 286.

10 Isaac ben Moses, *Sefer Or Zarua*, 4 vols. Zhitomir 1862, Vol. 1, No. 747, p. 213.

11 E. E. Urbach, *The Tosaphists: Their History, Writings and Methods*, Jerusalem 1980, pp. 433, 526–527.

12 Hayim ben Rabbi Yitzhak, *Responsa*, No. 221, p. 72.

13 A Rabbinic edict prohibiting a man from marrying more than one woman or from divorcing a woman against her will. See S. Goldin, *Jewish Women in Europe in the Middle Ages: A Quiet Revolution*, Manchester 2011, pp. 99–105.

14 Rashi at *Pesahim* 87a s.v. *ve-malhu*; b. *Bava Batra* 75a; *Midrasch Tehillim (Midrash on Psalms)*, ed. S. Buber, Wilna 1892 [repr. Jerusalem 1966], No. 145. Like R. Yehudah ben Moshe ha-Cohen, this expression is also used by *Yalkut Shimoni*, a midrash written during this same period, *Yalkut Shimoni*, Vol. 1, Jerusalem 1980, No. 888.

15 S. Baranfeld, *Sefer HaDemaot*, 3 vols. Berlin 1924–1931, Vol. 1, pp. 299–305, Vol. 3, p. 332; Salfeld, *Das Martyrlogium des Nürnberger Memorbuches*, pp. 329–331; A. Haberman, ed., *Sefer Gezerot Ashkenaz ve-Zarfat*, Jerusalem 1945, pp. 176–178. R. Yehudah ben Moshe ha-Cohen wrote *Va-etonen va-ekonen marah ve-alyah*; R. Shmuel ben Avraham wrote *Aishev bekhi va-nehi*. See Goldin, *Jewish Women in Europe in the Middle Ages*, pp. 39–42.

16 *Teshuvot uPsakim*, p. 170.

17 *Mordechai Ketubot*, No. 286.

18 The text begins with the word 'last year,' that is, the discussion is occurring during the course of the first year following the event. Asher ben Yehiel, *Shut haRosh*, ed. S. Yudelov, Jerusalem 1994, No. 32 §8.

19 *Mordechai Kiddushin*, No. 568

20 It is not clear when this inquiry and response were written, nor by whom. Urbach conjectures that the questioner was R. Joseph of Orleans Bekhor Shor, and that the respondent was someone called Rabbenu Tam. This places the question and answer in the middle of the twelfth century or shortly thereafter. The reasons given are not convincing and the answer does not reflect the opinion of Rabbenu Tam, as we shall see below. Urbach, *The Tosaphists*, pp. 132–133.

21 The source begins with the words: 'I found in *Sefer ha-Pardes* in the responsa of Rashi, of blessed memory,' but there is no trace of this responsum in the extant edition of *Sefer ha-Pardes*. It nevertheless seems to me that the source

was written by Rashi. See *Mordechai Ketubot*, No. 286; Blidstein, 'The Personal Status of Aposta†e,' pp. 58–59.

22 In this respect, he differs from Rav, whose remarks were directed, in my opinion, to men and not to women.

23 *Mordechai Ketubot*, No. 286.

24 In the source that disagrees with R. Ya'akov ben Meir, Rabbenu Tam, there appear the initials *Rib'am*, which may also refer to the name R. Yitzhak ben Meir; if so, we have here a dispute between two brothers, Rashi's grandsons. However, this interesting detail does not change the time frame of the discussion. See Tosafot *Ketubot* 3b s.v. *ve-lidrus lahen*.

25 Tosafot *Ketubot* 3b s.v. *ve-lidrus lahen*.

26 Tosafot *Ketubot* 3b.

27 Shlomo ben Isaac (Rashi), *Responsa Rashi*, ed. I. Elfenbein, New York 1943, No. 171. Rashi cites a woman who 'became a convert for a long time and was forbidden to her husband, and after some time returned to practice the ways of Judaism. She needed a *get*, but her husband was elsewhere.' Rabbi Yoel ha-Levi was asked whether a Jewish woman who went voluntarily with an idolater and stayed there three days in his home, and was then removed with a bribe, was permitted to return to her husband. He answered that she was permitted to return to her husband, in Isaac Ben Moses, *Sefer Or Zarua*, Vol. 1, No. 61; *Mordechai Ketubot*, No. 286. R. Isaiah di Trani, *Teshuvot RID*, Jerusalem 1967, pp. 285–286, No. 58. See A. Haverkamp, 'Baptised Jews in German Lands during the Twelfth Century,' in: *Jews and Christians in Twelfth Century Europe*, eds. M. A. Signer and J. Van Engen, Notre Dame, Ind. 2001, pp. 269–273 (and notes 98–115).

28 Moses of Zurich, *Sefer haSemak miZurich*, ed. I. J. har-Shosanim, 3 vols. Jerusalem 1973, Vol. 2, p. 120, No. 233; Urbach, *The Tosaphists*, pp. 509–510.

29 Meir ben Baruch, *Sheelot u-Teshuvot ha-Maharam*, Prague edition, No. 1,020; Meir ha-Kohen, *Teshuvot Maimuniut* to Moses ben Maimon, *Mishneh Tora*, Jerusalem 1952, *Hilcho Isurei Biaha* No. 18 [a].

30 Meir ben Baruch, *Sefer Sharei Teshuvot Maharam b. Barukh*, ed. M. A. Blakh, Berlin 1891, No. 80, pp. 117–188; Blidstein, 'The Personal Status of Apostate,' pp. 99–100.

31 A. Agus, ed., *Responsa of the Tosaphists*, New York 1954, s. v. 126, 127, pp. 235–237.

32 Numerous references to this problem appear in Judah b. Samuel he-Hasid, *Sefer Hasidim*, ed. J. Wistinetzki, Frankfurt am Main 1924, see Nos. 1,900, 1,898, 1,097.

33 Ya'akov ben Meir, *Sefer haYasharle Rabbenu Tam: Heleq haShe'elot vehaTeshunot* (Responsa), ed. S. F. Rosenthal, Berlin 1898, s.v. 25–26, pp. 42–45; Ya'akov ben Meir, *Sefer ha-Yashar* (News), ed. S. Schlesinger, Jerusalem 1959, pp. 448–449; Tosafot *Gittin* 34b s.v. *vehu*; Urbach, *The Tosaphists*, p. 121; Blidstein, 'The Personal Status of Apostate,' pp. 86ff.

6

Alternative perspectives:
The literature of pietists
(Ashkenazic *hasidim*)

The halakhic responses examined in the previous chapters are not only what is required for a discussion of the issue of self-definition. From a methodological viewpoint, we also need to examine issues and attitudes pertaining to mentalities that are not exclusively halakhic, by whose means we may also view the attitude towards those who abandoned the Jewish religion.

The book *Sefer Hasidim*, written during the first half of the thirteenth century, reflects the ideology of a small movement within the Jewish communities of Germany at the end of the twelfth and the beginning of the thirteenth centuries known as 'Ashkenazic Hasidism.'[1] Opinions differ as to the degree of involvement and influence this group exerted upon the Jewish community in general; however, even if it was an elitist group, it had explicit ambitions in the area of leadership, and its writings addressed different levels of the Jewish community. In terms of our present discussion, the sources and manner of writing of this group are very important, as they reflect moods and approaches that are not given expression in the mainstream of halakhic writings, and express substantive and significant mentalities. Ideologically, Ashkenazic Hasidism strongly emphasized the ability to withstand trials as a central component in the self-definition and self-fashioning of the Jew in general, and of the *hasid*, or 'pietist,' in particular, against whom its followers pose the 'regular' Jews and the 'wicked.'

The description of the apostate, or *mumar*, is expressed in *Sefer Hasidim* on three levels. On one level, the problematic reality at the end of the twelfth and the beginning of the thirteenth centuries is fully reflected as one in which there were many Jews who had converted to Christianity and yet remained within the environment of the Jewish group. We hear of apostates who had converted and lived in proximity to the community, at times even inside the community alongside their families who remained Jewish. Sometimes they even sought to participate in the activities of the community itself—for example, in funding the writing of a Torah scroll. They are perceived as a dangerous and negative element, who attempt to persuade Jews to become Christians and denounce Jews to the Christian authorities. The Jewish group felt contempt for them and was wary of their presence; they refer to them with contemptuous and insulting names, and refrain from mentioning their names even if their children are called to the reading of the Torah, or from quoting words of Torah that originated with them.[2]

On the second level, the ideology of Ashkenazic Hasidism, together with the construction of its self-consciousness and identity, is seen as the opposite to that of the apostates. The world is divided into three types of people: 'the ordinary person,' 'the wicked one,' and 'the pietist.' The *hasid* is a person capable of confronting tests and standing up to them; hence, he also withstands the temptation involved in conversion to Christianity. The 'ordinary person' may be tempted, and one may assume that he will not withstand the trial. It is for his sake that one needs to prepare means of atonement and return to Judaism. The 'evildoer' is the apostate, the person who has completely failed to stand up to the test and was seduced by Christianity on three separate dimensions—he was seduced by idolatrous religion; the opportunity to fulfill illicit sexual desire; and the possibility of eating anything he wishes.[3] In principle, according to the values of Hasidism, one must accept a Jew who has sinned and become a Christian and now wishes to repent; should he choose to return to Judaism he is treated like any other Jew (i.e., his wine is not considered *yayin nesakh*— i.e., pagan wine unfit for drinking—and he is not required to immerse himself in the *mikveh*). Notwithstanding, heavy duties are imposed upon him so that he may begin the process of *teshuvah* (repentance). First of all, and before all else, he must return to Judaism those whom he converted to Christianity, even if this will subject him to danger, quite literally; until that point, 'he is not taken back' for 'how can his transgressions be atoned?' That is, by its very nature atonement depends upon the correction of the harm he has caused.[4]

On yet a third level, we find the attitude towards the apostate as one of deep hostility and contempt. He is seen as blemished; the Jewish essence of the apostate is one that was substantially affected by his contact with Christianity, harming and damaging him in future stages of his life, even should he return to Judaism.[5] Harmful apostates are compared to such traitors from within the Jewish people as, according to the midrash, King

Ahab, who was referred to as an 'apostate out of appetite.' The Rabshakeh, who served as a messenger of Sennacherib in order to destroy Jerusalem was, according to the midrash, likewise an apostate Jew. The negative attitude towards him derives from the arrogance implicit in his daring to tell the Jews what God thinks of His people. In the Middle Ages, the answer to such an apostate was found, according to *Sefer Hasidim*, in the words of the prophet Isaiah: 'Shame on you, scorn on you, O virgin daughter of Zion; they wag their heads after you, O daughter of Jerusalem' (2 Kings 19:21–22).[6] But the principled approach of this book is even more extreme. Jeremiah 22:9–10—'Because they forsook the covenant of the Lord their God and bowed down to other gods and worshipped them. Do not weep for the dead and do not bemoan him. But weep for those who have gone astray, for they shall no longer return nor see his native land of his birth'—is interpreted as referring to an apostate who died as a Christian and whose relatives considered mourning him. The moment he converts one must lament and mourn for him, as if he had died, 'for he shall no longer return, but he is dead.' This argument negates the possibility that the apostate will return to Judaism.[7] Here, for the first time, we encounter the view that Christianity creates a blemish in the very essence of the person— or that perhaps the one who converted to Christianity already suffered a 'genetic' (hereditary) blemish in his family's past, and therefore his conversion was predestined. This approach, which is diametrically opposed to the one that took shape in the days of Rabbenu Gershom Meor ha-Golah and Rashi, effectively gives up completely on anyone who has converted to Christianity: his essence was already blemished and therefore there is no reason to invest in his return, given that if he does return his essence will remain unchanged and he is likely to cause harm to other Jews—whereas if he remains a Christian it is possible to be wary of him and he can no longer cause harm. In any event, rather than attempting to bring him in, he is pushed further away, and rather than emphasize that his historical essence is unchanged, emphasis is placed on his blemished nature.

These points are underscored repeatedly in the stories in *Sefer Hasidim*. The 'Sage' (i.e., the figure who gives all the good advice in the book), who perceives that parents are attempting in every possible way to return their converted son to Judaism, advises the parents not to attempt to bring him back. The Sage knows that the youth intends to persuade his brothers and sisters to follow the same evil path, and he also knows that when he was among Jews he caused them to eat non-kosher food ('he threw *treif* meat into the pot'). In other words, the Jewishness of the convert was blemished even before his conversion to Christianity, casting doubt upon the benefit likely to ensue (particularly to his family!) as a result of his return to Judaism. According to the Sage, if prior to his conversion he tried to make his family transgress, there is no reason to believe that after he returns things will be any better. The Sage suggests that something in the essence of the convert to Christianity is corrupt; hence, there is no point in attempting to bring him back to Judaism. The verse on which the author of *Sefer Hasidim* constructs his argument emphasizes his basic approach: 'Ephraim is addicted to images, let him be' (Hosea 4:17). The prophet advises the tribe of Judah to separate itself from the tribe of Ephraim because 'he is addicted to images'—that is, he has worshipped idols (the word *'atzavim* refers to idolatry, as in Psalm 115:5)—even though Ephraim and Judah were brothers. The halakhic authorities debate the question as to whether a Jew who has converted to Christianity has harmed the concept of brotherhood existing between Jews. The Ashkenazic *hasidim* assert that, in the case of a Jew who became a Christian, the concept of brotherhood never existed at all, even before he converted to Christianity.[8] Thus, too, in the story of the apostate who informs his community that he wishes to return to Judaism and to steal a large sum of money from the Christians to avenge himself on them, there are three responses. The first states, quite simply, that one who wishes to again be a Jew is forbidden to steal. The second relates to the character of the type of person who initially agreed to convert to Christianity, and discusses the process of atonement he must undergo (as we saw on the second level, above). A person who was overcome by his appetites (the appetite for money, the wish to eat pork, and the desire to violate the Sabbath) must, in undertaking repentance, adopt the opposite type of behavior: he must observe the Sabbath, refrain from eating pork, and take money from the Christians: 'and if they catch him and he is put to death, then his death will serve as atonement for all his sins.' The third approach advises not giving him any advice, and thereby not risking endangering the Jewish community. This is what they did in fact, and they were saved, because his true purpose was to defame the Jews.[9] In other words, there was a basic lack of trust in the convert to Christianity because of his presumed blemished nature; this story reflects the approach that his repentance was likewise false.

This process finds full expression in a passage cited in the name of Rabbi Judah he-Hasid on the Talmudic adage: 'The son of David will not come until all the souls within the body have been completed' (*b. Yevamot* 62a). He states that there is a chamber in the Heavens whose name is 'body' in which are concentrated all those souls given to human beings that will be born. The angel 'charged with pregnancy' places the soul within the body of the pregnant woman. At times the angel makes a mistake and places a soul intended to be in the body of a Gentile in the body of a Jewish woman, or vice versa. Such a soul will then belong to a person who in the end will convert to Christianity, while that soul which is intended to be a Jew but was placed in the body of a Christian woman will ultimately become a righteous Jewish proselyte.[10] In this manner, the process of change in the definition of consciousness and identity was completed: the Jew who became a Christian was not a Jew in his essence; rather, his soul was incarnated in a Jewish body by mistake, while in practice his soul was that of a Christian. Therefore, the fact that he abandoned his Judaism need not disturb us, as now the 'error' has been corrected and we may relate to him as he always was—namely, a Christian. Vice versa with regard to proselytes: the soul of the future convert to Judaism fell into the body of a Gentile by error, and by his act of conversion the Gentile with the Jewish soul restored the situation to what it should have been.

Notes

1 Y. Baer, 'The Religious-Social Tendency of Sepher Hassidim,' [Hebrew] *Zion* 3 (1938), pp. 1–50; H. Soloveitchik, 'Three Themes in *Sefer Hasidim*,' *Association for Jewish Studies Review* 1 (1976), pp. 311–357.

2 Judah b. Samuel he-Hasid, *Sefer Hasidim*, ed. J. Wistinetzki, Frankfurt am main 1924, Nos. 189–190 (p. 73), 511 (146), 604 (164), 790–791 (198), 1,424, 1,435 (345–347). See *b. Avodah Zarah* 46a.

3 Judah b. Samuel he-Hasid, *Sefer Hasidim*, Nos. 210 (p. 76), 189–190, 511, 208 (76). See: H. Ben Arzi, 'Asceticism in *Sefer Hasidim*,' [Hebrew] *Da'at* 11 (1983), pp. 39–46.

4 Judah b. Samuel he-Hasid, *Sefer Hasidim*, Nos. 208, 250 (pp. 82–83), 201 (75), 209 (76), 1,571 (336); J. Katz, *Exclusiveness and Tolerance*, Oxford 1961, pp. 93–105. It is thus that one may perhaps understand R. Eleazar Ba'al ha-Rokeah of Worms, who perceives him as tantamount to a new proselyte, due to his weighty sins; likewise the approach of R. Meir the Maharam of Rothenburg, who is suspicious that the returned apostate may not have fully repented and will harm Judaism even further.

5 Judah b. Samuel he-Hasid, *Sefer Hasidim*, Nos. 198 (pp. 74–75), 1,522 (465), 210.

6 See Rashi 2 Kings 19:21–22, and on *b. Sanhedrin* 60a. Cf. Judah b. Samuel he-Hasid, *Sefer Hasidim*, Nos. 189–190, 791, 1,476.

7 Judah b. Samuel he-Hasid, *Sefer Hasidim*, No. 192 (73–74).

8 Judah b. Samuel he-Hasid, *Sefer Hasidim*, No. 183 (72).

9 Judah b. Samuel he-Hasid, *Sefer Hasidim*, No. 200 (75).

10 A. Agus, ed., *Responsa of the Tosaphists*, New York 1954, p. 286.

Converts to Judaism

The Jewish ethos sees the Jew as unique, by virtue of his being the offspring of the chosen group of people who left Egypt, stood at Mount Sinai, received God's Torah, and entered into an eternal covenant with God. This ethos constituted the foundation of the Jew's identity during the Middle Ages. The concept is expressed in the personality of the Jew and is transmitted in a direct and unmediated way to his descendants. Thus, only a Jew, himself the descendant of Jews, can recite the formula of the blessing 'Blessed are You, O Lord God, King of the Universe, who has sanctified us with His commandments and commanded us,' as a descendant of those who directly received the Torah from God, and were sanctified and commanded by Him. Only a Jew, as the descendant of Jews, can address God in prayer using the phrase 'our God and God of our fathers,' because God is indeed his God and the God of his ancestors. Similarly, he may thank God in the Blessing after Meals for giving him 'the goodly land which You promised to our forefathers,' because he is a direct descendant of those who stood at Sinai and received that promise. This approach is closely related to the attitudes examined during the course of this study, according to which the nature of the Jew is not subject to change; hence, even if he converts to Christianity and is now immersed in the impurity of the Christian religion, which is seen as tantamount to idolatry, he still remains a 'New Christian,' a Jew in essence. We have seen above how this statement, applied to an apostate, changes due to the influence of historical events. Did the attitude concerning one who joined the Jewish religion change in a similar manner?[1]

As soon as the proselyte joins the Jewish group, the halakhic definition found in b. Yevamot 22a applies to him: 'A proselyte who converted is like a newborn infant.'[2] The proselyte is thus born anew, and all his previous family connections are completely nullified. This perception of religious conversion as an act of death and rebirth is known in many other societies.[3] Therefore (at least in theory), a father and daughter who were converted may marry one another, the biological son of a convert does not inherit from his father, and biological relatives who converted may testify against one another in a Rabbinic Court. The halakhic logic is flawless: familial relationships are absolute only when they are within the Jewish framework. Even one who departs from Judaism and cuts himself off from it cannot sever his familial ties and remains within the ethnic family, which is part of his identity. By contrast, one who joins the ethnic family as a proselyte severs all of his previous family ties, which are nullified in an absolute way.[4] Nonetheless, already during the Mishnaic period it was clear that, even if a convert is seen as being born anew as a Jew, he is a different kind of Jew in that he is unable to use those liturgical expressions indicative of the connection between the Jew in the present and the chain of his ancestors going back to Sinai. His connection to God as based upon the relationship to God of the patriarchs (which does not exist) is different from that of other Jews, which derives from the ancestral relationship.[5]

As against that approach, in the Jerusalem Talmud another seemingly marginal approach takes shape, stating that both Jews and converts have a common father—the patriarch Abraham. As Abraham made the substantive jump from serving idols to believing in the one God, he is considered the paradigmatic convert, and he received from God the title 'the father of many nations' (Genesis 17: 5–6). Therefore, his children, the proselytes, may recite the blessings and express themselves liturgically like all other Jews. This approach seems marginal in comparison to the direction developed in the Mishnah, which emphasizes the difference of the proselyte within Jewish society. Moreover, in the framework of the Talmudic discussion regarding those things one must tell the prospective proselyte prior to his conversion, one of the *amoraim*, Rav Helbo, states that 'converts are as difficult to Israel as a sore'—this, in explanation of the verse in Isaiah 14:1: 'And aliens will join them and will cleave to the house of Jacob' (*b. Yevamot* 47b). It may be that during the period of Rav Helbo, a Babylonian who immigrated to the Land of Israel during the first half of the fourth century, the proselytes indeed constituted a problem. He was evidently exposed in Palestine to the fact that, after the Roman empire became Christian, heavy punishments were imposed upon those who converted to Judaism, to the extent of being sentenced to execution.[6] This aphorism continued to echo throughout the history of Judaism, and its various interpretations reflect the essentially suspicious attitude towards the newcomer. Rashi, at the end of the eleventh century, explains the term 'sore' by stating that proselytes

cause harm to Jewish society in three different ways: First, they are not
expert in the mitzvoth and lead innocent Jews astray; moreover, all of the
Jews pay for their mistakes. In addition, they disturb the ideal state within
the Jewish community in which 'All Israel are responsible for one another'
(*b. Sotah* 37b), a situation prevented because converts have become mixed
within Israel.[7] These comments of Rashi, brought as a gloss on the words
of the Talmud, reflect his opinion of the proselytes of his period, or at least
the fear and suspicion regarding those converts who attempted to enter the
gates of the Jewish people. The medieval sages, until the end of the twelfth
century, did not modify these harsh formulations.

It is not clear how widespread the phenomenon of conversion, i.e.,
of Christians who wished to join the Jewish camp, was prior to the
twelfth century. It may be that, until that time, joining the Jewish people
was perceived as a convenient transition to a quality, prestigious group.
The halakhic discussion concerning the acceptance of converts during
the Middle Ages relates strictly to the motivations of the prospective
proselyte; the worse the situation of the Jews, the stronger became that
note emphasizing the need for purity in the convert's intentions in joining
Judaism. During the course of this discussion two views took shape. The
one held that it is permissible to convert even someone whose intentions
have not been proven at present, as it may be assumed that in the final
analysis the conversion will be 'for the sake of Heaven.' Thus, for example,
a certain young woman came and wished to convert in order to marry a
Jewish man. The rabbis accepted this, relying upon the precedent of those
cases cited in the Talmud of people who converted out of fear, as in the
time of David and Solomon, or of Mordechai and Esther, or the famous
case of the man converted by Hillel.[8] The second approach holds that the
entire conversion depends upon proving the true intentions of the convert.
Rashi emphasizes in his commentary on the Talmud that 'accepting the
yoke of the commandments' is of the very essence of conversion. Likewise,
in Germany at the beginning of the twelfth century, Ra'avan, and other
Tosaphists in his wake, underscored that, alongside informing the potential
proselyte of the commandments, one must examine whether or not his
motivations are pure or whether there is some ulterior motive for the
conversion—in their language, if it was 'because of some cause.'[9] At the
end of the thirteenth century Mordechai ben Hillel states that, in his
opinion, one ought not accept a proselyte unless it is very clear that he
wishes to join the Jewish people without any ulterior motive. However, he
qualifies his words by saying: 'I have written that which seems to me to be
correct; and from my teachers this measure seems [right], but do not rely

upon my understanding.'[10] During the Middle Ages the rabbis interrogated potential converts thoroughly, and only if they were convinced that they were doing this in a sincere and innocent way did they convert them. Above and beyond the above-mentioned discussion, which may have been theoretical, the medieval Talmudic commentators elaborated at length upon the subjects of circumcision and immersion of proselytes; there is also extant a contemporary source describing the actual reality per se. R. Gershom bar Yaakov was a *mohel* (ritual circumciser) who lived in Germany during the thirteenth century and wrote a book on matters of circumcision. According to him, one must be meticulous regarding all stages of the ceremony: initially, one teaches the convert and warns him regarding the difficulties involved in Judaism and in observing its mitzvoth; thereafter he must be circumcised; following that he is immersed in water; and only then can he recite the blessing, 'Blessed art Thou … who has sanctified us with His commandments and commanded us concerning immersion'—by which he becomes a Jew. At the immersion itself three Rabbinic sages or distinguished members of the community must be present, serving as a court whose function is to witness the final stage of the entrance into Judaism. During its course (prior to the immersion itself), they again inform him of the 'light and serious mitzvoth, and their punishments and their reward.' He must accept these upon himself, and only then is he immersed in water. Rabbi Gershom testifies to a case in Mainz in which the convert was first immersed and thereafter circumcised, and it was ruled that he must be immersed a second time—that is to say, the details of the ceremony of transition were serious and valuable.[11]

The most striking change in the ideological attitude towards the proselyte appears at the end of the twelfth century: a change that may be traced to the writings of R. Yitzhak ben Moshe (Or Zaru'a) in northern France and of R. Eliezer ben Yoel ha-Levi in Germany.

First, the expressions relating to proselytes are greatly moderated. The negative Talmudic expression, 'Evil after evil will befall those who accept converts … converts are as difficult to Israel as a sore' (*b. Yevamot* 109b) is explained by R. Yitzhak as referring to those who accept converts indiscriminately and without examining whether or not their intentions are sincere. He supports this perception by means of a historical-value criticism against the fathers of the nation. He states that, because of the refusal of Abraham, Isaac, and Jacob to convert Timna, she became the concubine of Eliphaz son of Esau, from whom was born Amalek, whose entire purpose was to harm Israel (*b. Sanhedrin* 99b). Thus, Amalek was the punishment visited upon Abraham, Isaac, and Jacob because of their refusal to accept as

convert a woman who wished to attach herself to the people of Israel. On
the other hand, he stresses the positive role played by Joshua, who accepted
Rahab the harlot as a convert, by Naomi, who accepted Ruth the Moabite as
a convert, and by Hillel the Elder, who accepted as proselyte the man who
said 'Convert me so that I can be the High Priest' (b. *Shabbat* 31a). In other
words, he emphasizes those cases in which people acted to accept converts
and succeeded, as against those in which they rejected potential converts
and failed.[12] Similarly, during this period the Tosaphists greatly modified
Rashi's words concerning those who convert others. The expression,
'Proselytes are as difficult to Israel as a boil' is explained as reflecting a
positive perception of proselytes: in their view, converts are 'difficult for
Israel' because the Torah warns in twenty-four separate places that one
must not harm them or cause them pain or oppression;' because Israel is
scattered about the world, and as a result many converts join their nation;
and because converts are meticulous in observing the commandments and
remind those who are born Jews to what extent they are not careful about
the mitzvoth.[13] That is, the seeming criticism of proselytes is reinterpreted
in a positive direction.

Second, R. Yitzhak also changes the halakhic approach concerning the
convert. He is firmly opposed to the decision of Rabbenu Tam regarding
the inheritance of the proselyte. He rules that a convert who has been
circumcised but, for whatever reason, was not immersed, and lived for a
lengthy period of time in the home of Jews, does not render their wine
non-kosher—i.e., he is no longer considered as a Gentile. He further
emphasizes that, if a woman converted while pregnant and then gave birth,
there is no need to immerse the infant in the *mikveh* for conversion, he is
simply circumcised like any other Jewish infant. R. Yitzhak also rules, with
great sensitivity, that if a person converted together with his mother and she
later died, that he may mourn for her. This decision is opposed to halakhic
logic, which strongly emphasizes that a convert is born anew, hence his
previous biological connections no longer exist.[14]

At the end of the twelfth century in Germany, R. Eliezer ben Yoel
ha-Levi (Rabya'li) heralded the change in attitude towards the convert. If,
in the case of R. Yitzhak, we need to conjecture as to the reason for the
change, in R. Eliezer ben Yoel ha-Levi we find the departure from previous
views expressed far more clearly. R. Eliezer ben Yoel ha-Levi was deeply
impressed by the quality and religious devotion of those Christians who
decided to convert to Judaism. He describes with great emotion a certain
proselyte, 'R. Abraham son of Abraham,' who underwent the transition
from Christianity to Judaism in Speyer, then went to his own city (evidently

Cologne), where he lived with the local Jews for a considerable period of time and learned the way of life of the Jews, the Hebrew language, and the Jewish Scriptures. When R. Eliezer saw that this convert was using a Latin Bible in order to understand the Hebrew in the Pentateuch, he explained to him that it was forbidden to learn the Torah in a language other than Hebrew. R. Abraham answered him that his 'rabbis' in Speyer, those who had converted him, taught him that this was acceptable. Thus, despite his principled misgivings, R. Eliezer ben Yoel ha-Levi came to the conclusion that he was allowed to read the Torah 'in the script of the monks,' because of the special situation in which both the Jews and the proselytes found themselves. (R. Eliezer ben Yoel ha-Levi's position was based upon the midrashic interpretation of the verse, 'It is time to act on behalf of the Lord, they have violated Your Torah'—Psalms 119:122.) When R. Eliezer ben Yoel ha-Levi heard that the inhabitants of Würzburg did not allow R. Abraham to serve as prayer leader while staying in their city, due to the ruling in *Tractate Bikkurim* that a convert, rather than saying 'God of our fathers' must say 'God of the fathers of Israel' or 'God of your fathers,' he wrote that in his day it was preferable to follow the ruling in the Jerusalem Talmud, stating that a convert is like a Jew in every respect because he is considered a son of the patriarch Abraham.[15]

This situation needs to be understood against the background of Jewish self-perception during the medieval period. So long as the convert ameliorates his own situation by converting, or there is the possibility that he will derive some sort of benefit from doing so, the Ashkenazic authorities were hesitant to accept him, and the suspicion of him remained. This intuitive suspicion of proselytes is based upon the self-perception which sees Jews in the present as the direct descendants of the Jews who stood at Mount Sinai, enjoying direct contact with God via the Torah; against them are all those who wish to join or penetrate this exclusive group. The attitude towards proselytes began to change as the situation of the Jews became more difficult, as the number of Jews who converted to Christianity grew, and as the danger to one who converted to Judaism was also exacerbated. The Christian who joined the Jewish group lost all of his property, and even placed his very life in danger. The criterion for joining the Jewish group became the danger to life this entailed, his martyr-like behavior facilitating a new value-perception of the convert. The 'people of Israel' saw itself as a distinct, extended family, beginning with the patriarch Abraham, and continuing on via his preferred son Isaac, and Jacob, the preferred son of Isaac, to the creation of the nation with all of its tribes, the sons of Jacob, who stood at Mount Sinai at the time of making the eternal covenant with God. The emphasis upon the shared genealogical origin of the people of Israel, which constructs the people as a single unit deriving from its common ancient ancestors, whose direct descendants allude to them in prayer, makes it difficult to accept the proselyte. He has no common father and no common essence with other Jews, beginning with the patriarchs and taking shape at Mount Sinai. In the Middle Ages, this tension was intolerable, and therefore the patriarch Abraham was called upon to bridge it.[16]

Already in the chronicles depicting the death of Jews as martyrs in the First Crusade, first written at the beginning of the twelfth century, there stands out the behavior of a convert in the town of Xanten who asks the most distinguished member of the community whether he, as a proselyte, can enter Paradise after dying a martyr's death. The very posing of the question testifies to the fact that the proselyte lived with the feeling of being different from his Jewish 'brethren.' In his responsum, R. Moshe ha-Kohen marshals the words of Rav Judah from the Jerusalem Talmud, written seven hundred years earlier: 'As Abraham is the father of the proselytes, you may enter Paradise with all the righteous and with Abraham.' Note the presence of other proselytes in the list of those who died as martyrs in Cologne. Particularly interesting is the figure of Rabbi Yaakov ben Rabbi Sulam who, because his father belonged to a family that 'was not honorable,' took a proselyte as his wife. He commented to all those around him that for his entire life people had treated him with contempt, but that now he was dying a distinguished martyr's death.[17]

The use of the figure of Abraham in connection with proselytes is decisive on two levels: Abraham became the first 'convert' when he turned from the worship of idols to the belief in the One God. By this act he endangered his life, was thrown into the fiery furnace, and saved by God. Abraham is also the archetype of one who converts others, according to the traditional interpretation of the verse 'and the souls which he made in Haran' (Genesis 12:5), according to which the word 'souls' refers to 'the proselytes whom he converted.'[18] It is thus that Abraham appears in midrashic and in medieval literature: as a figure who was reborn, who abandons pagan religion, and who endangered his life by the very act of conversion. Thus also are depicted those Gentiles who converted when they saw the spiritual heroism of Daniel's three companions, Hananiah, Mishael, and Azariah. Isaiah 29:24—'And those who err in spirit will come to understanding, and those who murmur will accept instruction'—is taken as referring to those Gentiles who are present at manifestations of the greatness of the God of Israel, join the people of Israel, and become 'understanding' and 'accept instruction.' These include Jethro, Rahab, and the other converts to Judaism in the wake of the action of Hananiah, Mishael, and Azariah.[19]

The name 'son of Abraham' was given to every proselyte as his patronym, thereby designating that he had been born anew; in the Middle Ages the image of the proselyte also included the subject of martyrdom. From this stage on, whenever the threat of martyrdom appears, proselytes are able to carry their new name with pride, with the confirmation of the Jewish society around them, and they are called 'Abraham' or 'the son of Abraham.' In one of the memorial books, at least three proselytes are listed, of whom two came from the world of the Church, all of whom died as martyrs for Kiddush Hashem. In the memorial book, in the list related to the city of Weissenburg, we find:

1. Rabbi Abraham son of Abraham (our Father) from France, who was 'the head of all the barefoot ones,' who became disgusted with the images and took shelter in the shadow of the Eternal Living One, and was burned for the Unity of the Name. He evidently lived at the end of the twelfth century, and is the person mentioned in Tosafot, alongside R. Yitzhak.

2. Rabbi Abraham ben Abraham from Augsburg, who was disgusted with the god of the nations and cut off the heads of the images and trusted in the Life of the Universes, and underwent severe sufferings and was burnt for the Unification of the Name on Rosh Hodesh Kislev, which was a Friday, 'in the 25th year of the sixth millennium [i.e., 5025],' 21 November 1264.

3. Rabbi Yitzhak ben Abraham Our Father from Würzburg was burned for the Unification of the Name.[20]

In 1264 or 1265, a proselyte named Avraham was burned at the stake in the city of Augsburg or Weissenburg. The description of his acts corresponds to that of the patriarch Abraham as described in the midrash. Like Abraham, this convert was willing to die for his new faith and was put to death by fire by the Christians. Two liturgical poems (*piyyutim*) written in his honor and to commemorate his martyr's death are extant; it would appear that these poems were used on the memorial day for this proselyte martyr. The *piyyut*, *Mah rav tuvkah* ('How Great is Your Goodness'), was composed by R. Mordechai ben Hillel, the close disciple of Rabbi Meir of Rothenburg and author of the most comprehensive commentary on the Talmud of his day, who himself died as a martyr.[21]

The author asks God to end the period of Exile and bring the Redemption, and emphasizes how loyal the Jews are to their God, that they do not sin and, primarily, that they are willing to sacrifice themselves in order to demonstrate that they cannot be made to change their religion. The example he cites to prove this is that of Avraham the proselyte, and the Jewish inhabitants of the city Sinzig. He emphasizes the identity between the patriarch Abraham and Avraham the proselyte.

Avraham the proselyte is perceived here as virtually identical to Abraham himself, the first proselyte and the father of all proselytes, and he now becomes 'a sweet fragrance, a burnt-offering of service on the mountain where the Lord shall be seen'—that is, a sacrifice offered on Mount Moriah, where Abraham bound his son Isaac (Genesis 22:14), following a tradition that was established in the *piyyutim* from the time of the First Crusade. The city of Sinzig is Mount Moriah, and the Jews who died there for Kiddush Hashem, including the proselyte, are compared to Isaac. From the perspective of Rabbi Mordechai there is no difference between the proselyte and the Jewish martyrs. The comparison between the proselyte who chose to forego his life as a Christian and the other Jews is based upon a reconstruction of the transition of the proselyte from his life as a Christian to that as a Jew, based upon the example of Abraham in the midrash, which describes the transformation from Abraham the idolater to Abraham the Hebrew. Abraham identifies the falsehood involved in the worship of idols and discovers faith in the one God, smashes the idols, and is brought to trial before King Nimrod, who orders him to be thrust into the fire in order to prove whether his God is really the true God. Abraham enters the inferno and is miraculously saved. R. Mordechai describes the thirteenth-century proselyte Avraham, who arrived at the conclusion that Judaism was the true religion, as defining the religion from which he had come as a false and idolatrous one and, like Abraham, he 'broke the idols of Christianity.' Also like Abraham, he understands that the Christian god is 'wood and stone'—pagan, created by human beings; he was circumcised at an advanced age; and he arouses discussion when he engages in polemics with the idolaters (Christians) concerning the nature of the true God. Like Abraham, he wanders here and there in order to continue his Jewishness; and he is caught and taken to be executed by fire.

In this liturgical poem, we accompany the proselyte as he is taken to be executed, wrapped in *tallit* and *tefillin*. Prior to his death he is questioned about his faith (he may have been asked this by Church officials in the hope that he would recant and confess his sins before being executed), and he answered, 'Know to whom this *tallit* and these *tefillin* belong'—that is, the proselyte. Just before his death by fire, he paraphrases the words used by Tamar in Genesis 38:25. Our author here uses the words said by Tamar in order to prove her righteousness and her unshaken faith, referring to the personal effects of Judah that were in her possession.'[22]

Rabbi Mordechai places in the mouth of the proselyte a clear attack against Christianity. When the proselyte says regarding circumcision, 'I have removed not only the foreskin of my heart, but also the foreskin of the flesh,' this is a protest against the words of Paul in the New Testament.[23] But the full expression of the inclusion of the proselyte within the people of Israel appears when the liturgical author applies to the proselyte the phrase 'by those close to Me I shall be sanctified' (Leviticus 10:3), the expression used by Moses to comfort his brother Aaron upon the death of his sons. The proselytes are those who are close to God, they are the exemplary Jews. In a second *piyyut*, R. Moshe ben Yaakov defines Abraham the proselyte in accordance with his faith and his deeds. He is prepared to be burnt alive rather than recant and believe in 'the hanged one'; he cuts himself off from the pagan world when he has himself been circumcised like Abraham.[24]

Notes

1 J. M. Panitz, 'Conversion to Judaism in the Middle Ages: Historic Patterns and New Scenarios,' *Conservative Judaism* 36 (1983), No. 4, p. 46; A. Reiner, 'L'attitude envers les proselytes en Allemagne et en France du XIe au XIIIe Siecle,' *Revue des études juives* 167 (2008), pp. 99–119.

2 *b. Yevamot* 22a, 48b, 62a, 97b. This expression only appears in the Babylonian Talmud. In the Jerusalem Talmud, there is another expression, 'A Gentile has no father.' The former expression indicates the proselyte's complete break with the connection to his biological past. The second expression expresses doubt regarding familial relationships among Gentiles from the outset, but it is not directly relevant to the present discussion. M. Lavie, '"A Convert is Like a Newborn Child": The Concept and its Implications in Rabbinic Literature' [Hebrew], PhD Thesis, Ben-Gurion University of the Negev 2003, pp. 49–57.

3 A. Van Gennep, *The Rites of Passage*, London 1960, pp. 91–92; M. Eliade, *Rites and Symbols of Initiation: The Mysteries of Birth and Rebirth*, New York 1965, pp. 28–37 and in the introduction.

4 The permission in principle for a mother and son or brother and sister who have converted to marry one another is of course strictly theoretical. The sources stress that this is not a real option, lest it be said that those who convert to Judaism do so in order to commit incest!

5 *m. Bikkurim* 1.4.

6 A. Linder, *Roman Imperial Legislation on the Jews* [Hebrew], Jerusalem 1983, pp. 53–57.

7 Rashi in *Yebamot* 47b s.v. *deamar mar*, 119b s.v. *kashim gerim*, *Niddah* 13b s.v.

ke-saphat, Sanhedrin 27b s.v. *ella be-pashol*, 39b s.v. *mipnei ma*, to Exodus 30:7. Tosafot *Niddah* 13b s.v. *kashim*.

8 Tosafot *Yebamot* 24b s.v. *lo bymei David*.

9 Rashi in *Yebamot* 47b. Rashi adds here to that which appears in the Talmud and, in characteristic fashion, states that at the time that the Temple was standing, the convert was also required to bring a sacrifice, and if he did not do so the process of conversion was incomplete. See also Tosafot *Yebamot* 24b s.v. ולא בימי דויד; Eliezer ben Nathan, *Sefer Even haEzer, Sefer Ra'avan*, Jerusalem 1984, 242b; and in Moses of Coucy, *Semag: Sefer Mizvot Gadol*, Jerusalem 1961.

10 *Mordechai Yebamot*, No. 100. During the fourteenth century R. Yaakov ben Asher (Ba'al ha-Turim), emphasizes that all converts are accepted, notwithstanding ulterior motives—see *Tur, Yoreh De'ah* 268.

11 Jacob and Gershom the Circumcisers [Hagozer], *Sefer Zikhron Brit*, ed. J. Glassberg, Berlin 1892, p. 133.

12 Tosafot *Yebamot* 109b s.v. *raha tahat raha*.

13 Tosafot *Kiddushin* 70b s.v. *khashim.*

14 Ya'akov ben Meir, *Sefer ha-Yashar* (Responsa), ed. S. Rosenthal, Berlin 1918, No. 51. See Tosafot *Bava Batra* 140a; Tosafot *Yebamot* 47b–48b and 109b, Tosafot *Kiddushin* 17b and 70b, Tosafot *Avodah Zarah* 64b; *Mordechai Mo'ed Katan*, Nos. 907–908. See Reiner, 'L'attitude envers les proselytes,' pp. 99–119.

15 Eliezer ben Joel ha-Levi, *Sefer Ra'aviah*, ed. V. Aptowizer, 5 vols. Jerusalem 1983, 2008, Vol. 2, *Megillah* 549.

16 G. Porton, *The Stranger Within Your Gates*, Chicago 1994, pp. 194–195; M. Lavie, '"A Convert is Like a Newborn Child,"' pp. 103–105; M. Lavee, 'Converting the Missionary Image of Abraham: Rabbinic Traditions Migrating from the Land of Israel to Babylon,' in: *Abraham, the Nations, and the Hagarites: Jewish, Christian, and Islamic Perspectives on Kinship with Abraham*, eds. M. Goodman, G. van Kooten, and J. van Ruiten, Lieden 2011, pp. 203–222.

17 A. Habermann, ed., *Sefer Gezerot Ashkenaz ve-Zarfat*, Jerusalem 1945, pp. 49, 35, 103; S. Salfeld, *Das Martyrlogium des Nürnberger Memorbuches*, Berlin 1938, p. 9.

18 *Midrash Bereshit Rabba*, Jerusalem 1965, Noah 38:13.

19 *Midrash Bereshit Rabba*, 39:1, p. 365; *MidrashShir ha-Shirim Rabbati*, ed. S. Dunski, Jerusalem 1980, *Parasha* 1; *Yalkut Shimoni*, Vol. 2, Jerusalem 1980, *Shir ha-Shirim* No. 981; Abraham bar Azriel, *Sefer Arugat ha-Boshem*, ed. E. E. Urbach, 3 vols. Jerusalem 1939–63, Vol. 2, p. 122, note 11.

20 Salfeld, *Das Martyrlogium des Nürnberger Memorbuches*, p. 22; Habermann, ed., *Sefer Gezerot Ashkenaz ve-Zarfat*, p. 186.

21 I. Davidson, *Thesaurus of Medieval Jewish Poetry* [Hebrew], 4 vols. New York 1970, Vol. 3, p. 96, No. 604.

22 See Rashi at Genesis 38:25; the phrase 'wear glory' in Ezekiel 24:16 alludes to the *tefillin*. Actually both Tamar and Abraham were thrown into the burning fire, and both were saved. *Tefillin*—phylacteries; *tallit*—prayer shawl.

23 E.g., Romans 2:25–29; 4:9–12. About the Christian view on circumcision see D. Bell, *Sacred Communities*, Leiden 2001, pp. 60–69.

24 This poem as well is derived from midrashim which were familiar in the Middle Ages, see *Midrash Tanhuma*, ed. S. Buber, Jerusalem 1964; *Yalkut Shimoni*, Vol. 2, Samuel No. 162.

8

Conclusions: The change in mentality

Jewish self-definition in medieval Europe was based upon classical Jewish values: first, the eternal covenant between God and the Jewish people as the chosen people; second, an explicit Jewish identity deriving from the world of commandments unique to Judaism. As the Jewish group lived within Christian society, the essence of whose theological view was that Christians and Christianity had supplanted Jews and Judaism as God's chosen people and religion, the Jewish group made efforts to emphasize, in its own self-definition, the difference between itself and the society at large. As a result, one of the elements of the Jewish self-definition was its self-understanding as being 'non-Christian.' That is, it was not only the positive values that characterized the Jew as such that entered into the scale of values, the process of socialization, the ceremonies and prayers, but also the negation of that which was defined as its opposite. The Jew defined himself first and foremost as a Jew, and thereafter as a 'non-Christian.' The more successful was the Christian society, the more confident it was in itself and in emphasizing characteristic values derived from Christianity; the Jewish self-definition, in corresponding fashion, emphasizes its own values, defining them as explicitly Jewish and underscoring their difference from those of the surrounding Christian world. The Jewish self-definition was based upon a self-image as 'good,' 'pure,' 'innocent' (in the sense of 'whole' or 'complete'), but also upon such values as 'not evil like the Christian,' 'not impure like the Christian,' and so on; this same scale of values was likewise emphasized with regard to the religion and its symbols.[1] Since Christianity declared its desire to convert the Jew to Christianity by means of economic temptation, theological persuasion, and even by violent coercion, Jewish efforts concentrated upon intensive processes of socialization in order to protect itself against these attempts.[2] Thus, among all the forms of (social) deviation, the most serious was that involved in conversion from one religion to another. For the Jewish group that lived within a Christian society that emphasized its religious superiority, its physical and theological victory, and its perception that, whatever might happen, in the final analysis the Jews would indeed accept the Christian truth, the conversion of an isolated individual was perceived as a theological disaster, an affront to morale and hope, and a constant threat.

With regard to mentality, the terminology used is of very great importance, as it influences both the popular perception and the individual's perception of the other. The popular folk perception tends to portray the convert to Christianity in somber or ridiculous light, thereby shaping and strengthening the self-definition that completely negates the act of deviance itself. Every negative term emphasizes the opposite of that term as being of value, superior, and special. Regarding those who converted to Christianity, the most basic term used was *meshumad*, or 'apostate,' a harsh term describing the convert to Christianity as one who had undergone a process of destruction (from the Hebrew root *shm'd*, destroy; see above, Chapter 1). Rashi, in describing the convert to Christianity, uses the term 'alien son, uncircumcised of heart' (Exodus 12:43; Ezekiel 44:9), explaining that 'his deeds are alien to his Father in Heaven, and they are uncircumcised of heart; it is one whether he is a Gentile or an apostate Jew.'[3] Rashi, whose principled approach regarding the expectation that the apostate will recant underlies his halakhic understanding of the convert to Christianity, notes that by his deeds the apostate had destroyed his relationship with God and thereby lost his identity, which was close to God, in both a spiritual and a physical manner—something had happened to his heart. This is doubtless a reaction to the Christian view that sees one who has converted to Christianity as undergoing a 'change of heart'—a conversion. In the act of circumcision which a Jew undergoes at the age of eight days, a covenant, whose physical expression is in the removal of the foreskin, is made between the Jew and his God. The Jew who accepts Christianity has not undergone a 'change of heart,' as the Christians claim, but a process of sealing off or closing of his heart. The convert to Christianity takes the impure foreskin, removed from him at his Brit as a symbol of purification, and returns it to his heart. There is no conversion of the heart but, to the contrary, the convert to Christianity is now 'uncircumcised of heart'; his heart is closed, impure.

The self-characterization of the Jew in the Middle Ages as 'pure' and 'righteous' is in stark contrast to the definition of one who has joined Christianity as being impure in his very essence. Generally speaking, the

Jewish writings describe the motivation of the convert to Christianity in terms of surrender to his lower, animalistic, sexual instincts. There is no acknowledgement that these Jews may have been convinced by the Christian theological truth, or by the beauty or physical majesty of Christianity. Rabbi Yitzhak ben Moshe (Or Zaru'a), in the thirteenth century, takes a term from the Talmud in order to describe the convert 's subjugation to his physical appetites, using the expression 'one who deliberately gives himself an erection' (*maksheh atzmo la-da'at*) as tantamount to 'apostate.' R. Ami, in the Talmud, describes the type who becomes addicted to the pleasures of the flesh: 'For thus is the guile of the Evil Urge: today it says to you 'Do this,' and he does so, and tomorrow it says 'Go worship idols,' and he goes and worships them.' R. Ami, who lived in the Land of Israel during the third century, refers to this type as a 'transgressor'; R. Yitzhak ben Moshe in thirteenth-century Christian Europe refers to him as 'an apostate.'[4]

The severest attitude is reserved for those elements within Jewish society that were perceived as weakest. On the one hand, they need to be cultivated so that they do not break, but they must also be defined as a potential danger. An example of this is found in the behavior towards children. As I have shown in my study of the attitude towards Jewish children in the Middle Ages in Christian Europe, Jewish children are the subject of a proprietary, concerned, and fashioning attitude during this period. They are smothered with physical affection, there is sensitivity to their physical vulnerability, and great attention is given to their education. They will be attacked in the future by the Christians; they are the first target of Christian missionary efforts. The Jews are concerned that they will be captured and taken by force and raised as Christians.[5] Therefore, as much as the attitude towards them is caring and positive, it is also harsh and distancing in the event that these efforts fail and the children become Christians, even against their will.

We have already noted that the attitude towards children whose parents abandoned Judaism and converted to Christianity was extremely harsh. The question asked in this context regarding a small child whose parents in practice converted him against his will—what difference does it make?—is a logical one. The answer given is that, if he dies as a Christian and does not manage a return to Judaism, the attitude towards him does not take into account that Christianity was imposed upon him unknowingly. To the contrary, it is derived from the bare fact that he died as a Christian; it is a happy event that he died and did not continue his life as a Christian. While this is also the halakhic position of Rabbenu Tam, it is rooted in a mentality of competition for those Jews whom the Christians, from the Jewish point of view, had tried to convert in missionary fashion. The halakhic decision here derives from the mental attitude towards this competition. The power with which it dismissed the sympathetic attitude that might have been expected towards the exceptional case of a child who died after his parents had converted him to Christianity without his understanding, is symptomatic of the negative attitude towards the convert to Christianity generally, who died as a Christian and did not recant of his 'error' while still alive. Notwithstanding the halakhic justification, the perspective is one of mentality.[6]

In societies under siege, such an attitude derives from the need to strengthen those who, in the eyes of society, are perceived as weak sub-groups within it. The attitude towards women is similar.

The woman is perceived as representing the ability of the community to stand up for its values. The woman is perceived in an ambivalent manner: on the one hand she is seen as strong and representative, but at the same time as weak and easily persuaded or influenced. In Jewish descriptions of Christian violence directed against them during the First Crusade, and the Christian attempts to convert them to Christianity even by force and by means of threats upon their lives, the woman appears at the forefront of active opposition to forced conversion, and among those who turned to the path of martyrdom 'for Kiddush Hashem'; they are an example inspiring the men not to convert to Christianity even under coercion or duress, and even merely for appearance, acting decisively to sacrifice their very lives. These descriptions are not ones that the men initiated in order to strengthen the feminine image. We learn, from the memorial lists, that the women died in the same numbers as the men during the course of the twelfth century. Women preferred not to convert with their husbands but to remain Jewish, even if this might create difficulties for them in the future. Nevertheless, the male mental perception saw the women as an element which could not, under any circumstances, be allowed to be broken, placing upon them the power and fortitude of the community as a whole. Thus, if women were kidnapped, or broke down and converted for appearances, there developed a harsh and problematic perception of them, as I have analyzed in detail in Chapter 5.

During the course of the tenth and eleventh centuries, the confident self-definition of the Jew distinguished him in a superior way from the Christian world. A Jew who converted to Christianity did not express, according to the Jews, the victory of Christianity, but only the weakness of that particular Jew. He was tempted, he was weak, and the Jews expressed their absolute confidence that he would sooner or later return to the Jewish truth. For Rabbenu Gershom Meor ha-Golah, at the beginning of the eleventh century, and for the authors of the chronicles of the First Crusade, who wrote at the beginning of the twelfth century, there is a distinct tendency to polemicize with those who converted to Christianity, based on a perception that they would be convinced by the writing and the arguments and return to Judaism. It is possible to discern this optimistic perception in the *piyyutim* (liturgical poems) written by Rabbenu Gershom, as well as in sections from the chronicles written close to the time of the disaster that befell the Jews during the First Crusade. These passages were written for Jews who had been tempted, who had made a mistake, who were forced to convert to Christianity, and now refuse to return to Judaism or try to enjoy the best of both worlds. These writings argue with the decision of these former Jews, out of the assumption that if one were simply to explain to them in a suitable manner the facts of life and the eternity and purity of Judaism as against the wickedness and impurity of Christianity and the ludicrousness of their claim that God had regretted His earlier choice and decided to transfer his favor, these former Jews would understand and return to Judaism.

This tendency disappeared entirely during the thirteenth century. The books of polemics written during the thirteenth century were written for internal Jewish consumption, and were intended less, if at all, to persuade Jews who had converted to Christianity. In *Sefer ha-Vikuah* of Yosef ha Mekane there is, it is true, a section that discusses verses in Latin taken from the New Testament. This may have been addressed to Jewish apostates who attempted to convince Jews who remain Jews using 'proofs' from the New Testament. But it is more likely that the verses constituted a framework for theological negation of the arguments of Christian missionaries directed against Jews, or as proofs of the crookedness and foolishness of Christian belief, for Jews who knew Latin and were in contact with Christians. Towards the end of the thirteenth century, this element was also missing from the polemical writings. It would seem that the Jews by this time did not consider it necessary to invest much effort in bringing back Jews who had converted to Christianity. They had redefined them, and themselves.

At the end of the tenth century and the beginning of the eleventh century, Rabbenu Gershom Meor ha-Golah attempted to organize a *takkanah* (Rabbinic edict) to prevent Jews from mentioning the past to those who had converted to Christianity and returned in repentance to Judaism; and to prevent those Jews who had remained Jews from referring to a former apostate with negative or insulting names. He did this so that apostates would not hesitate to return to Jewish society out of fear that they would be accepted badly or in an insulting manner by their Jewish brethren. It is almost certain that, during the age of Rabbenu Gershom, those who had converted and subsequently returned to Judaism were harmed and subjected to insulting terms by other Jews. Rabbenu Gershom Meor ha-Golah, as leader, attempted to combat this phenomenon; it may have been of particular importance to him because of his son's conversion to Christianity; in any event, it is clear that he saw his *takkanah* in terms of the need to return the former converts to their Judaism.

Subsequently, this edict seems to have been completely forgotten. Thus, during the first half of the thirteenth century Rabbi Yitzhak ben Moshe, 'Or Zaru'a,' does not know at all of such a *takkanah*. Rabbi Yitzhak ben Moshe came from the East and stayed for a lengthy period of time in northern France, studied in almost all the famous centers of learning in France, then went to Germany, and there too he went from one yeshiva to another in order to learn with most of the central Jewish teachers of the mid-thirteenth century. Yet R. Yitzhak ben Moshe does not know at all of such a *takkanah*. He sees conversion to Christianity as a shameful thing, which he describes in the words, 'a shame and a scandal for his children.' If a person is referred to with insulting names, it is the task of the judges of the community to decide how to deal with him, as someone who has shamed his fellows. But there is no emphasis upon any special protection of one who had converted and returned. The attitude towards the convert to Christianity no longer derives from the wish to prevent his being insulted because this might prevent him from returning to Judaism. The attitude towards the apostate ceased to be a problem of the 'Jewish entity' and simply became a matter of insult as such.[7] The significance of this is simple: the Jewish group sees the convert to Christianity as one who has betrayed his Judaism, whose essence has been harmed, and it no longer awaits his speedy return, his acknowledging his error, and his thereby strengthening Judaism's theological victory. This approach finds expression, of course, in the halakhic aspects of what the the Jewish leaders decided to impose upon the apostate who wishes to return to Judaism.[8] Moreover, beyond the intricacies of the halakhic discussion, we can see and understand the mental approach in which, on the folk level, the apostate is seen as a traitor to his people, and from this moment on as one who is not deserving to be, or to be considered as, a Jew, even in his hidden Jewish essence, until such time as he returns to Judaism.

The most substantial change is found at the end of the thirteenth century, in the writing of R. Meir ben Baruch (Maharam) of Rothenburg, particularly in his overall substantive statement regarding the convert to Christianity, one that radically alters the decisions of Rabbenu Gershom Meor ha-Golah, and of Rashi from the end of the eleventh century in France. R. Meir ben Baruch of Rothenburg explains this new view in relation to a woman who had married a Jewish man who died, and now needs to receive *halitzah* (release from potential levirate marriage) from his brother who has become a Christian. Rashi stated that in such a case the woman requires *halitzah* and, being aware of the Geonic responsum that states otherwise, stated explicitly that it was impossible to rely on this Geonic ruling. R. Meir ben Baruch of Rothenburg and his disciples completely uproot this decision of Rashi,[9] adhering to the view that lay at the basis of the Geonic decision—namely, that if at the time the couple was married the brother of the bridegroom, i.e., the *yabam*, had already changed his religion, and thereafter the husband died leaving no offspring, his wife is not required to receive *halitzah* from her brother-in-law. R. Meir ben Baruch of Rothenburg strengthens the stance of the Geonim against that of Rashi on the basis of a 'proof' brought from *Tractate Bava Kamma* (110b), concerning the possibility that a condition which is not articulated explicitly, i.e., an 'implied condition,' can nevertheless be used to nullify a contract. According to the Talmud, it is difficult to accept such a halakhah, for that would enable an easy solution for the problem of a woman whose husband died and whose *yabam* suffers from boils. There, too, we could argue that at the time of the marriage there was an implied condition that, should the husband die, the marriage would be retroactively nullified, for certainly no woman would want to live with a person suffering from boils. The Talmud rejects this argument by saying that a woman would in fact prefer to be married, even to a husband with boils, rather than to be left alone and single. R. Meir ben Baruch of Rothenburg infers from this that, in such a case, where the *yabam* suffers from boils, the woman would prefer to live with him (rather than to be left by herself), but that this is not the case where he had converted his religion. In that case, life shared with him would be opposed to halakhah because of the suspicion that the apostate husband would influence his new wife to change her religion, and indeed we find extensive Jewish activity involving cases in which the husband converts and his wife remains Jewish, in which the community takes concerted actions to separate them.[10] In such a case, therefore, one may invoke the argument of implied condition, and assume that, had the woman known at the time of her marriage that her husband would die and that she would need to marry his apostate brother, she would not agree to such a marriage and it is considered as nullified from the outset. This is R. Meir ben Baruch of Rothenburg's argument. However, the question arises that R. Meir's argument is only valid where the brother in fact converted prior to the marriage, so that already then she could have foreseen the possibility that her husband would die and she would need to marry his brother. But in fact, in the case under discussion, the brother converted after the couple's marriage. Hence, it is not reasonable that the woman could imagine that her brother-in-law would convert to Christianity, and therefore we do not have here even an implied condition. But despite this argument, the author of the response claims that, even if the conversion had taken place while the couple was already married, one could still argue that there was an implied condition. Thus Rabbi Abraham ha-Gadol asks: In the case of a *yabamah* (childless widow), who falls before an apostate for *halitzah,* does she need to receive *halitzah* from him and is she considered a married woman so long as her apostate brother-in-law has not granted *halitzah*? R. Yitzhak ben Moshe of Vienna, the Or Zaru'a, writes: It is written in the response of Rav Nahshon Gaon and in the book *(Basar) al ha-Gehalim*, and in the response of many other authorities, that if a *yabam* was an apostate at the time of his brother's marriage and is still an apostate, his sister-in-law is exempt from the obligation of receiving *halitzah* and is allowed to marry whomever she wishes. Moreover, this halakhah applies even if the apostate brother returned to Judaism after the husband's death because at the time that her husband was still alive, his wife assumed that she would never agree to live with her apostate brother-in-law, and it is as if this condition was already explicit at the time of the marriage. According to Rabbenu Hananel, this rule applies even if the brother was a practicing Jew at the time of his brother's marriage but converted prior to his brother's death: he does not give *halitzah* and does not perform *yibbum* (levirate marriage), and his sister-in-law may marry whomever she wishes.

The position held by Rashi, which relates in principle to the concept that the apostate remains a Jew in his essence, changed in light of the approach of the halakhic sages of the end of the thirteenth and beginning of the fourteenth centuries. R. Abraham ha-Gadol and Rabbenu Hananel think that the woman in our case is allowed to marry *ab initio*, without *halitzah*. In other words, they do not accept the view that the apostate's essential Jewishness was not altered by his conversion to Christianity. Even according to those who adhered to the stricter view of Rashi prohibiting such a woman from marrying, would accept such a marriage retroactively. Nevertheless, we find a great deal of unease among the judges, who waver between the approach of Rashi and those views brought at the end of the thirteenth century. The son of R. Yitzhak ben Moshe received an angry letter on this subject at the end of the thirteenth or the beginning of the fourteenth century, in which its authors urge him to examine the writings of his father and tell them, finally, his father's position so that they may know how to decide:

> Behold, I appeal to you a second time regarding the matter of a woman who has a levir dependence upon an apostate *yabam*, who already converted at the time she was married, according to the words of our French rabbis. And your words to us are too brief, for you did not clarify to us whether our Teacher and Master, your father, decided in his book according to the words of those who are permissive or not, for we did not understand his reasons.[11]

In other words, in principle they accepted the view of R. Meir ben Baruch of Rothenburg and found a way to justify it from a halakhic viewpoint. In the final analysis, during the fifteenth century this problematic situation was corrected by ruling that, if the bridegroom had a brother who had converted to Christianity, a condition was made at the time of the marriage that, 'should she fall before an apostate for *halitzah*, the marriage is retroactively annulled.'[12] The hope lying at the basis of Rabbenu Gershom Meor ha-Golah's approach, i.e., that there was a possibility that the apostate might return to Judaism, and Rashi's view that one did not forego the Jewish essence of the convert to Christianity, had completely disappeared.

As we have seen, during the thirteenth century people depicted the figure of the person who had converted to Christianity not as one who had committed an error, nor as one who had been seduced by bodily temptations and appetites, but rather as one who had been convinced by Christianity and, especially, as one who intended to harm Judaism in a severe manner. His Jewish past, and at times also his expertise in Jewish writings, gave him destructive potential as one who intended to harm, and often did harm, the very essence of Jewish existence in the Christian world. Rabbi Moses of Coucy in France, and R. Meir ben Menahem and R. Yedidya, who all remembered the horrible experience at the time of the burning of the Talmud in Paris, as the result of the acts of an apostate, understood and described this personality—the zealous apostate. The damage which this zealous apostate wished to cause derived from his profound understanding of the central views of the Jewish people and its hopes, and it was precisely these fundamentals that the apostates wished to harm. They fully deserved the uncompromising appellation they were given by members of what was formerly their people—*meshumadim* (literally, 'destroyed ones'). Donin wished to harm the halakhic heart of Judaism—the Talmud. He deliberately ignored the usual Christian direction of theological debate with the principles of Judaism, and the attempt to achieve a theological victory in polemics, directing his arrows against what he saw as the embodiment of the very soul of the Jewish people. It is that which he wishes to harm—and does.

And indeed, at the end of the thirteenth century, when R. Meir ben Baruch of Rothenburg attempted to initiate an 'Exodus' of the Jews from Germany after having identified a substantive change in the attitude of the imperial rulers towards the Jews, 'he sets out on a journey eastward,' evidently in the direction of the Land of Israel. An apostate Jew identifies him and brings about his arrest and prolonged imprisonment. The potential for harm on the part of the apostate Jew, which R. Meir ben Baruch of Rothenburg identified well from the moment of his own terrible experience with the apostate Donin which led to the burning of the Talmud, manifested itself in an ironic and bitter manner on himself, and an apostate Jew was able to halt the most important act of R. Meir ben Baruch of Rothenburg, his attempt to extract his community from Germany—and the Jewish community saw this.

It should be emphasized that the apostate's advice to the emperor was to take R. Meir ben Baruch of Rothenburg captive as the Jewish community certainly would not allow him to wallow in prison and would redeem him for whatever sum of money the emperor might impose upon them. It is explicitly stated that 'the king [emperor] believed the apostate' and he put R. Meir ben Baruch of Rothenburg in prison. But the latter ordered his fellow Jews not to pay an excessive amount for his release, but only a relatively small amount of money. As a result he remained imprisoned for seven years, until he died in prison. In the end, a certain Jew ransomed his body for an enormous sum, asking only that after his own death he be buried near R. Meir ben Baruch of Rothenburg. To this day it is possible to see the double graves, adjacent to one another, at the entrance to the ancient Jewish cemetery in Worms. The story is recorded on the gravestones for future generations. Every Jew who enters the cemetery sees the two tombstones containing the well-known story of the treacherous behavior of the apostate Jew against a prominent Jewish leader. In the middle of the seventeenth century, Rabbi Yuzfa Shemesh writes that 'a certain apostate informer denounced him to the King of Rome.'[13] It is this perception that accompanies the Jewish apostate from Rothenburg's time onwards, and it finds expression in the growth of folk stories literature.

Towards the end of the thirteenth and the beginning of the fourteenth centuries, we find a substantial change in the folk literature related to apostasy. During this period one begins to find legendary traditions intended to explain and to rationalize the conversion to Christianity of important figures in medieval Jewry, such as the sons of Rabbi Shimon bar Yitzhak 'ha-Gadol' and that of Rabbenu Gershom Meor ha-Golah. In these writings (first published at the beginning of the seventeenth century, in 1602), we find a new attitude towards the conversion to Christianity of Elhanan, son of R. Shimon bar Yitzhak, an extraordinary eleventh-century *paytan* (liturgical poet).[14] Elhanan was kidnapped from the Jews as a small child by a Christian woman, who gave him to the Church to raise him. He was a talented child, and so successful in the Church that he became pope. From this high office he understood the extent to which Christianity was mistaken and succeeded in establishing renewed contact with his Jewish father. There are various different endings to the story: he succeeds in fleeing and lives secretly in Worms; he nullifies an edict that had been imposed upon the Jews; he dies as a Jew, sanctifying the Great Name, and his father includes his name in a liturgical poem.[15] This folk story portrays the conversion of Jews to Christianity, their ascent to high levels within the Christian Church, and, upon reaching the pinnacle of the hierarchy, their being motivated to take care of those Jews who remained in the community or to die as a Jewish martyr. Such a story is an important vehicle for explaining the deviant behavior of Jewish converts to Christianity. The clear message is that Elhanan had a 'Jewish' goal in his deviant behavior: his deviant behavior not improper behavior that weakens the position of the original group, but rather emphasizes the ability of the minority group to succeed in causing theological harm at the central weak point of the rival religion. The Jew who succeeds in deceiving the forces of Christianity succeeds at the same time not only in saving his Jewish community, but also to show that the religion to which he had converted is not the true religion, and that he, as the son of an important Jew, was never truly convinced by the Christian religion—not even as pope!

There likewise emerged a legend concerning the conversion to Christianity of the son of Rabbenu Gershom Meor ha-Golah. According to this folk legend from the beginning of the fourteenth century, Rabbenu Gershom wrote the *piyyut*—'My throat is hoarse from crying out against violence / I have seen the wicked ones allowing the holy to be trod down / Hear my cry and let the day of vengeance come'— after his son had thrown his Prayer Book to the ground in the middle of Yom Kippur, left the synagogue, and converted to Christianity.[16] When his wife saw his great pain, she disclosed to him that once, on the night that she returned from the *mikveh*, she had been raped by a Christian horseman, and that this child was the result of the rape. As proof that this had been a violent rape and that she tried to resist to the best of her ability, she kept the earlobe which she bitten off her assailant in the middle of the struggle 'and Rabbi Gershom's mind was quieted.' Of course, the story is a-historic and non-halakhic, flavored with the detail of the ear that had been bitten off as a symbol of 'the maiden who is raped and cries out and none hears.' Moreover, it bypasses any halakhic discussion of the issue of the rape, for if the woman is raped the son is in fact considered to be that of the putative father, her husband.[17]

During the eleventh century, in the age of Rabbi Shimon and Rabbenu Gershom, Jewish self-identity was so self-evident that it was impossible to refute it through stories of converts to Christianity. However, during the centuries that followed, the Jews experienced a religious crisis that led to certain cases of willing conversion to Christianity; there were apostate Jews who caused their brethren great harm in every realm, so that their self-confidence progressively declined in light of this phenomenon. The representation of the convert to Christianity as one who was undeserving from the outset to be considered as part of the Jewish people made it easier to accept this phenomenon, particularly as it was accompanied by that of proselytism, of Christians of a high level who were prepared to join Judaism. The ultimate test for a Jew, that of martyrdom, was now carried out by proselytes, former Christians who were prepared, at the cost of their own lives, to prove that Judaism was victorious and that the view that one was to oppose Christianity to the point of death was stronger than the tolerant view that a Jew who had deviated and become a Christian nevertheless continued to be defined as a Jew as long as he lived.

These two folk legends clearly exemplify those approaches that emerged in light of the phenomenon of conversion to Christianity by Jews. The first story shows that the Jew who converted to Christianity did not really convert; the second emphasizes that the Jew who converts to Christianity was not a 'pure Jew.' In this respect, the second story is similar to passages we have found among the Ashkenazic *hasidim*, stating that the soul is at times misplaced within the wrong body; thus, the soul of the son of Rabbenu Gershom Meor ha-Golah was not a Jewish soul. It is self-evident that, in order to complete the discussion of converts to Christianity from the twelfth through the fourteenth centuries, we must now examine the mirror image that was developing at the same time—the phenomenon of conversion to Judaism.

Just as the Jewish group redefined its attitude to apostates in light of historical developments, so too did it with regard to those who converted *to* Judaism. As acts of martyrdom, of death for Kiddush Hashem increased, and the view that one ought to kill oneself and not convert to Christianity, not even to the mere appearance of it, became the dominant one; and as the number of those who willingly converted to Christianity increased, and particularly when these Christianizers began to cause concrete harm to the Jewish community, the attitude towards converts to Christianity became extremely negative and their halakhic definition as 'brethren' was greatly weakened. As the situation of the Jews became increasingly difficult, and as it became more dangerous for a Christian to convert to Judaism, the attitude towards proselytes likewise changed. They began to be perceived as people who were preparing themselves for a martyr's death by the very fact of their conversion, and as dying a martyr's death in the literal sense when they were caught and willing to die rather than to return to Christianity. While this phenomenon already appeared at the time of the First Crusade, as we have seen, it did not find its full expression until the end of the twelfth century, and even more so during the course of the thirteenth century, which was an exceedingly difficult period for the Jews. In the consciousness of the Jews, the proselyte was the polar opposite of the convert to Christianity. He was adorned with expressions of endearment, while the convert to Christianity was called an 'apostate,' an expression of distance and alienation. The proselyte had cast off the pagan world, while the convert to Christianity took that world upon himself. The proselyte was prepared to die as a martyr for his faith, while the apostate to Christianity lost his faith and his world, and harmed the Jews.

From the fourteenth century on, there were an increasing number of examples of Jews who converted to Christianity and attempted to cause harm to their former coreligionists. This damage might consist of simple things, such as attempts to damage the Sabbath *eruv* (the symbolic boundary around the Jewish community enabling Jews to carry objects from one place to another), thereby making it very difficult for Jews to function in their community on the Sabbath. Harming the *eruv* was an act whose aim was to cause nuisance to the Jews and make it difficult for them to celebrate their holy day in a peaceful and convenient manner. If a Gentile damaged the *eruv*, making it halakhically unfit, he did so because he wished to spoil something related to the Jews that was within 'his' urban space. A Jew who converted to Christianity and was familiar with the mechanism of the *eruv* and its importance in the life of the Jews damaged it out of a desire to strike a blow specifically at a point with which he was familiar.[18]

The most substantial blows against medieval Jews began with the publication of libels against them by Jews who had converted to Christianity.

Thomas of Monmouth, who publicized the story concerning the supposed murder by the Jews of the child William of Norwich (1144), begins with the assumption that the Jews indeed need to kill a Christian child, because he had heard this from an apostate Jew, Theobald of Cambridge.[19] The libel regarding Jewish desecration of the Host began in 1290 in Paris when an apostate Jew named Jean de Thilrode related the account, in the first person: a Parisian Jew named Jonathan purchased the sacred bread, the Host, from a Christian servant woman. Jonathan supposedly gathered the Jews together for the ceremony of profaning the Host. They attempted to divide the bread, but did not succeed. Thereafter the bread broke by itself into three parts and blood began to flow from it. When the Jews threw pieces of the bread into a pot of boiling water, the bread turned into a human being. Jean and his family immediately converted, blaming Jonathan and his family for the act. As a result he was arrested by the bishop of Paris and then executed.[20]

The harsh events of the pogroms of Rindfleisch and of Armleder (end of the thirteenth and beginning of the fourteenth centuries) began as the result of stories told by Jews who had converted to Christianity concerning a supposed Jewish plot to steal the Host and to profane it, just as they had done to the body of Jesus, and still attempt to do. The acts of slaughter referred to as Rindfleisch began as a result of such a libel started by apostates and involved more than 150 communities in southern Germany and Austria, where more than 20,000 people were murdered (the numbers vary between 20,000 and 100,000).[21]

In a detailed study by Miri Rubin of libels connected with the Host, she proves that apostate Jews were involved in almost every libel concerning Jews allegedly attempting to steal the Host in order to profane it or harm it. It was they who informed on the (supposed) acts of the Jews, and who reported in detail the tortures which the Jews performed upon the Host, and were the prize witnesses who reported the miracles performed by the Host which the Jews had attempted to desecrate. Between 1369 and 1370 an attempt was made to harm the new Jewish community in Brussels, and against the wealthy and noted Jew, Jonathan of Enghien. This was done by apostates, one of whom describes how the Jews obtained the sacred bread and how they harmed it. The second describes how Jonathan's wife persuaded him to smuggle the Host to Cologne. The Jews were dragged through the streets of Brussels and were then executed.[22] At the end of the fourteenth century, an apostate named Peter (formerly Pesah), who engaged in polemics with Rabbi Yom-Tov Lipmann-Muhlhausen, emphasized that the Jews sought the destruction of Christianity, harming the sanctity of the

Host in order to do so. As a result of this accusation, about eighty Jews who had been placed in prison were executed. Peter also explained the ritual of *bi'ur hametz*, the burning of remnants of leavened bread before Passover, as an anti-Christian act. Peter denounced the Jews, accusing them of horrible acts on the basis of his reliable knowledge as a former Jew. The burning of *hametz* before Passover is thus brought as a proof of the burning of the Host.[23]

One of the most dangerous personalities for Jews living in the middle of the fifteenth century was the Franciscan monk John of Capistrano, who was assisted in providing a basis for his anti-Jewish actions by a group of apostate Jews. He succeeded, in the course of a public debate, to convince an important Roman Jew to convert to Christianity; he brought about the expulsion of the Jews from Bavaria; he caused the suspension of Jewish privileges, and the restriction of their rights in Sicily. In 1453, he made use of the testimony of Jewish apostates against their former brethren for desecrating the Host, leading to the slaughter of the Jews of Breslau.[24] In the 1470s, Jewish apostates repeatedly informed on their former brethren, citing various acts of ritual murder of children or profaning the Host. In the majority of cases, imperial investigation revealed these accusations to be false, but on occasion Jews were nevertheless imprisoned or expelled.[25] At the beginning of the sixteenth century (Frankfurt, 1515), an apostate Jew accused the Jews of hanging the Host which they had stolen on the wall of the synagogue. During the second half of the sixteenth century in Italy, after the Counter-Reformation, the number of Jews who converted to Christianity and conveyed information about acts of the Jews increased. The most dangerous figure among these was Alessandro Francesca (Hananel de Polonia). Among other things, he reported, in the wake of the murder of a child in Rome in 1555, that 'every year, between Purim and Passover, the Jews are accustomed to murdering a gentile child.'[26]

What was the real place of the Jewish apostates within the overall complex of this story? Did the Christian authors choose to place them so clearly and centrally as those accusing their brethren in order to give a more serious, exact, and credible status to the stories of the horrors committed by the Jews? Was the place of the Jewish apostates so central in Christian writing because they were the central witnesses to the victory of Christianity? Did the Jewish apostates in fact inform on their erstwhile brethren because they attempted to harm the Host, sought to destroy the Christian world, and more? Generally speaking, this was in fact the case.[27] For example, during the first half of the sixteenth century, the apostate Antonios Margerita explained the songs of the Passover Haggadah as curses directed by the Jews against Christians and Christianity. The apostate Victor von Corbin tells of the liturgical poems for Yom Kippur in which the Jews curse the Christians.[28] The dissemination of these stories served the New Christians as an entrance ticket to the new world. Moreover, generally speaking there burned within them the fire of Christian faith, and they were convinced that they had the power to overcome their former brethren in polemics and to show them the light.[29]

From the Jewish point of view, this abandonment of Judaism was doubly treacherous. It was not only that the apostates attached themselves to the central impurity in the world; that they abandoned their brethren in their travails: even worse was the appearance of a group of 'former Jews' who sought to attack Judaism and succeeded, by exploiting their intimate knowledge of Judaism and the Jewish community to focus most effectively their attacks upon the central, substantive, painful point. In this respect, the apostate was seen as a disgusting and lowly figure, one whose return to Judaism was no longer awaited, and even though the old halakhic perception remained (i.e., if he wishes to return, he may do so, and he is to be accepted as a Jew), the popular image of him and his understanding within the Jewish mentality became that of the embodiment of evil.

Notes

1 A. S. Abulafia, 'Invectives against Christianity in the Hebrew Chronicles of the First Crusade,' in: *Crusade and Settlement*, ed. P. W. Edbury, Cardiff 1985, pp. 66–72.

2 My main field of research: S. Goldin, 'The socialisation for "Kidush ha-Shem" among Medieval Jews,' *Journal of Medieval History* 23 (1997), pp. 117–138; S. Goldin, 'Juifs et juifs convertis au Moyen Age: "Es-tu encore mon frére?," *Annales, Histoire, Sciences Sociales* 54 (1999), pp. 851–874; S. Goldin, 'Jewish Society under Pressure: The Concept of Childhood,' in: *Youth in the Middle Ages*, eds. P. J. Goldberg and F. Riddy, York 2004, pp. 25–43; S. Goldin, *The Ways of Jewish Martyrdom*, Turnhout 2008.

3 Rabbenu Gershom Meor ha-Golah related in his commentary to a *kohen* (a member of the priestly class) who became a Christian; Rashi explains this as referring to every Jew. See M. Perry, *Tradition and Transformation: Knowledge Transmission among European Jews in the Middle Ages*, Tel Aviv 2010, pp. 128–194. Rabbenu Gershom to *Thanit* 18a; Rashi to Exodus 12:43, 48; Rashi to *Sanhedrin* 22b; Moses of Coucy, *Semag: Sefer Mizvot Gadol*, Jerusalem 1961, Nos. 308, 353, 355.

4 Isaac ben Moses, *Sefer Or Zarua*, 4 vols. Zhitomir 1862, Vol. 1, No. 123; *b. Nidha* 13b. See the midrashic literature to Exodus 12:43.

5 Goldin, 'Jewish Society under Pressure,' pp. 25–43.

6 Goldin, 'Jewish Society under Pressure,' pp. 25–43.

7 Isaac ben Moses, *Sefer Or Zarua*, Vol. 1, No. 751.

8 As has been described recently by Kanarfogel articles. E. Kanarfogel, 'Returning to the Jewish Community in Medieval Ashkenaz: History and Halkhah,' in: *Turim, Studies in Jewish History and Literature Presented to Dr. Bernard Lander*, Vol. 1, ed. M. A. Shmidman, New York 2007, pp. 69–97.

9 Meir ben Baruch, *Sheelot u-Teshuvot ha-Maharam*, Prague edition, ed. M. A. Blakh, Budapest 1895, No. 1,022.

10 See Eliezer ben Joel ha-Levi, *Sefer Ra'aviah*, ed. V. Aptowizer, 5 vols. Jerusalem 1983, 2008, Vol. 5, No. 939; Moses of Coucy, *Semag: Sefer Mizvot Gadol, Ashin* No. 50; Tosafot Rosh *Gittin* 34b; Hayim ben Rabbi Yitzhak, *Responsa*, Leipzig 1860, No. 116.

11 Hayim ben Rabbi Yitzhak, *Responsa*, No. 114.

12 Joel ben Samuel Sirkis, *Bayit Chadash* on *Even ha-Ezer, Arba'ah Turim*, Jerusalem 1990, No. 157.

13 S. Eidelberg, *R. Juspa, Shammash of Warmaisa (Worms)*, Jerusalem 1991, pp. 78–82; Abraham ben Samuel Zacuto, *Sefer Yuhasin*, Königsberg 1858, p. 223.

14 Rabbi Shimon bar Yitzhak was referred to in the Middle Ages with such superlatives as 'a spring flows from his grave,' 'the master of miracles,' 'the Righteous,' 'of the seed of David,' 'the light of the Diaspora, who enlightened the Exile with his hymns.' The name Elhanan appears in the acrostic of a *piyyut* written by his father. See A. Grossman, *The Early Sages of Ashkenaz* [Hebrew], Jerusalem 1981, pp. 86–102.

15 J. Prinz, *Popes from the Ghetto*, New York 1968; see the translation of the legend pp. 17–20; A. Jellinek, *Beit ha-Midras*, 6 vols. Jerusalem 1967, Vol. 5, pp. xxxviii, 148–152; Vol. 6, pp. xxxiii, 137–139; *Ginse Nistaroth*, Vol. 3, ed. J. Kobak, Bamberg 1872, pp. 1–4.

16 A. Grossman, 'A Typological Legend about the Conversion of the Son of R. Gershom Me'or ha-Gola,' [Hebrew] in: *Studies in Jewish Narrative, Ma'aseh Sippur, Presented to Yoav Elstein*, eds. A. Lipsker and R. Kushelevsky, Ramat Gan 2006, pp. 65–75.

17 This detail appears in the commentary to this *piyyut*. Grossman, 'A Typological Legend,' p. 68, note 10. See *b. Sotah* 27a.

18 *Sefer Minhage R. Shalom bar Isaac*, Jerusalem 1997, No. 363.

19 *The Life and Miracles of St. William of Norwich*, eds. A. Jessop and M. R. James, Cambridge 1896, Book II, pp. 93–94; G. Langmuir, *Towards a Definition of Antisemitism*, Los Angeles 1990, pp. 224–226.

20 S. W. Baron, *A Social and Religious History of the Jews*, 18 vols. Philadelphia 1952–83, Vol. 11, pp. 168, 307–308; P. Browe, *Die eucharistischen Wunder des Mittelalters*, Breslau 1938, pp. 128–132; S. Simonsohn, *The Apostolic See and the Jews*, Toronto 1991, pp. 58–60, esp. note 54, p. 50; M. Rubin, *Gentile Tales: The Narrative Assault on Late Medieval Jews*, London 1999, pp. 119–128.

21 Baron, *A Social and Religious History*, Vol, 11, pp. 416–418; Simonsohn, *The Apostolic See and the Jews*, p. 60, esp. note 57; Rubin, *Gentile Tales*, pp. 119–128.

22 Rubin, *Gentile Tales*, pp. 181–182.

23 R. Yom-Tov Lipmann-Muhlhausen, *Sefer ha-Nizzahon*, Amsterdam 1827; I. J. Yuval, *Two Nations in Your Womb*, Berkely 2006, pp. 130–133.

24 Rubin, *Gentile Tales*, p. 85; Simonsohn, *The Apostolic See and the Jews*, pp. 71–74.

25 Rubin, *Gentile Tales*, pp. 129–131

26 Simonsohn, *The Apostolic See and the Jews*, pp. 281–286, esp. p. 285.

27 J. Elukin, 'From Jew to Christian? Conversion and Immutability in Medieval Europe,' in: *Varieties of Religious conversion in the Middle Ages*, ed. J. Muldoon, Gainesville, Fla. 1997, pp. 171–189.

28 Yuval, *Two Nations in Your Womb*, pp. 123, 130–131.

29 The new type, that of the apostate who delivered crippling blows to the community from which he had come, was of course a well-known phenomenon in Spain, as were the well-known apostates who tirelessly acted against their former brethren in order to convince them to convert to Christianity, such as Alphonso of Wallalid = Abner of Burgos; Paulus de Santa Maria = Shlomo Halevi; and Heronymus de Santa Feda = Joshua Halorki. Y. Baer, *A History of the Jews in Christian Spain*, 2 vols. Philadelphia 1961, 1966), Vol. 1, pp. 152–159.

Bibliography

Primary sources

Abraham bar Azriel, *Sefer Arugat ha-Boshem*, ed. E. E. Urbach, 3 vols. Jerusalem 1939–63.

Agus, A., ed., *Responsa of the Tosaphists*, New York 1954.

Aronius, J., *Regesten zur Geschichte der Juden im frankischen und deutschen Reiche bis zum Jahre 1273*, Berlin 1902.

Asher ben Yehiel, *Shut haRosh*, ed. S. Yudelov, Jerusalem 1994.

Baranfeld, S., *Sefer HaDemaot*, 3 vols. Berlin 1924–1931.

Davidson, I., *Thesaurus of Medieval Jewish Poetry* [Hebrew], 4 vols. New York 1970.

Eidelberg, S., *The Jews and the Crusaders*, the English translation of Habermann, *Sefer Gezerot Ashkenaz ve-Zarfat*, Madison 1977.

Eidelberg, S., *R. Juspa, Shammash of Warmaisa (Worms)*, Jerusalem 1991.

Eliezer ben Joel ha-Levi, *Sefer Ra'aviah*, ed. V. Aptowizer, 5 vols. Jerusalem 1983, 2008.

Eliezer ben Nathan, *Sefer Even haEzer, Sefer Ra'avan*, Jerusalem 1984.

Eliezer ben Samuel of Metz, *Sefer Yere'im*, Vilna 1901.

Gershom ben Judah [Meor ha-Golah], *Selihoth u-Phizmonum*, ed. A. Habermann, Jerusalem 1944.

Gershom ben Judah, *Teshuvot Rabbenu Gershom Me'or haGola*, ed. S. Eidelberg, New York 1956.

Ginse Nistaroth, Vol. 3 ed. J. Kobak, Bamberg 1872.

Habermann, A., ed., *Sefer Gezerot Ashkenaz ve-Zarfat*, Jerusalem 1945.

Haverkamp, E., *Hebraische Berichte uber die Judenverfolgungen wahrend des ersten Kreuzzugs, Monumenta Germaniae historica. Hebraische Texte aus dem mittelalterlichenDeutschland*, Hannover 2005.

Hayim ben Rabbi Yitzhak, *Responsa*, Leipzig 1860.

Isaac ben Moses, *Sefer Or Zarua*, 4 vols. Zhitomir 1862.

Jacob and Gershom the Circumcisers [Hagozer], *Sefer Zikhron Brit*, ed. J. Glassberg, Berlin 1892.

Jellinek, A., *Beit ha-Midras*, 6 vols. Jerusalem 1967.

Judah b. Samuel he-Hasid, *The Life and Miracles of St. William of Norwich*, eds. A. Jessop and M. R. James, Cambridge 1896.

Judah b. Samuel he-Hasid, *Sefer Hasidim*, ed. J. Wistinetzki, Frankfurt am Main 1924.

Mahzor Vitry, ed. S. Horowitz, Nuremberg 1892.

Meir ben Baruch, *Sefer Sharei Teshuvot Maharam b. Barukh*, ed. M. A. Blakh, Berlin 1891.

Meir ben Baruch, *Sheelot u-Teshuvot ha-Maharam*, Prague edition, ed. M. A. Blakh, Budapest 1895.

Meir ha-Kohen, *Teshuvot Maimuniut* to Moses ben Maimon, *Mishneh Tora*, Jerusalem 1952.

Midrasch Tehillim (Midrash on Psalms), ed. S. Buber, Vilna 1892 [repr. Jerusalem 1966].

Midrash Shir ha-Shirim Rabbati, ed. S. Dunski, Jerusalem 1980.

Midrash Tanhuma, ed. S. Buber, Jerusalem 1964.

Mordechai ben Hillel, *Sefer Mordechai*, in editions of the Babylonian Talmud.

Moses of Coucy, *Semag: Sefer Mizvot Gadol*, Jerusalem 1961.

Salfeld, S., *Das Martyrlogium des Nürnberger Memorbuches*, Berlin 1938.

Shlomo ben Isaac (Rashi), *Sefer ha-Ora*, Vol. 2, ed. S. Buber, Lemberg 1905.

Shlomo ben Isaac (Rashi), *Responsa Rashi*, ed. I. Elfenbein, New York 1943.

Teshuvot uPsakim, Responsa et Decisiones, ed. E. Kupfer, Jerusalem 1973.

Ya'akov ben Meir, *Sefer ha-Yashar* (Responsa), ed. S. Rosenthal, Berlin 1918.

Ya'akov ben Meir, *Sefer ha-Yashar* (News), ed. S. Schlesinger, Jerusalem 1959.

Yalkut Shimoni, Vol. 1, Vol. 2, Jerusalem 1980.

Yehiel ben Joseph, *Vikuah* [Dispute], ed. R, Margulies, Lvov 1928.

Yom-Tov Lipmann-Muhlhausen, *Sefer ha-Nizzahon*, Amsterdam 1827.

Yosef b. Natan Official, *Sefer Yosef ha Mekane*, ed. J. Rosenthal, Jerusalem 1970.

Zidkiya ben Abraham, *Sefer Shibolei haLeqet*, Vol. 1, Vol. 2, Jerusalem 1961, 1969.

Secondary sources

Abulafia, A. S., 'Invectives against Christianity in the Hebrew Chronicles of the First Crusade,' in: *Crusade and Settlement*, ed. P. W. Edbury, Cardiff 1985, pp. 66–72.

Abulafia, A. S., *Christians and Jews in the Twelfth-Century Renaissance*, London 1995.

Adler, M., *Jews of Medieval England*, London 1939.

Aronius, J., *Regesten zur Geschichte der Juden im Frankischen und deutschen Reiche bis zum Jahre 1273*, Berlin 1902.

Baer, Y., 'The Disputation of R. Yehiel of Paris and of Nahmanides,' [Hebrew] *Tarbiz* 2 (1931), pp. 172–187.

Baer, Y., 'The Religious-Social Tendency of Sepher Hassidim,' [Hebrew] *Zion* 3 (1938), pp. 1–50.

Baer, Y., *A History of the Jews in Christian Spain*, 2 vols. Philadelphia 1961, 1966

Bell, D., *Sacred Communities*, Leiden 2001.

Ben Arzi, H., 'Asceticism in Sefer Hasidim,' [Hebrew] *Da'at* 11 (1983), pp. 39–46.

Ben-Sasson, H. H., *Continuity and Variety* [Hebrew], Tel Aviv 1984.

Berger, D., *The Jewish-Christian Debate in the High Middle Ages: A Critical Edition of the Nizzahon Vetus*, introduction, translation and commentary D. Berger, Philadelphia 1979.

Blidstein, G. J., 'Who is not a Jew? The Medieval Discussion,' *Israel Law Review* 11 (1976), pp. 369–390.

Blidstein, G. J., 'The Personal Status of Apostate and Ransomed Women in Medieval Jewish Law,' [Hebrew] *Shenaton ha-Mishpat ha-Ivri* 3–4 (1976–77), pp. 35–116.

Blumenkranz, B., *Juifs et Chretiens dans le monde accidental 430 –1096*, Paris 1960.

Blumenkranz, B., 'Germany 843–1096,' [Hebrew] in: *The Dark Ages*, ed. C. Roth, Tel Aviv 1966, pp. 62–74.

Blumenkranz, B., 'Jüdische und Christliche Konvertiten im jüdisch-christlichen Religions gespräch des Mittelalters,' in: *Judentum im Mittelalter: Beiträge zum christlich-jüdischen Gespräch*, ed. P. Wilpert, Berlin 1966, pp. 264–283.

Bonfil, R., 'The Cultural and Religious Traditions of French Jewry in the Ninth Century, as Reflected in the Writings of Agobard of Lyons,' in: *Studies in Jewish Mysticism Philosophy and Ethical Literature*, eds. J. Dan and J. Haker, Jerusalem 1986, pp. 327–348.

Boshof, E., *Königtum und Königschersschaft im 10 und 11 Jahrhundert*, Munich 1993.

Browe, P., *Die eucharistischen Wunder des Mittelalters*, Breslau 1938.

Browe, P., *Die Judenmission im Mittelalter und die Päpste*, Rome 1942.

Carlebach, E., *Divided Soul*, New Haven 2001.

Chazan, R., 'The Blois Incident of 1171: A Study in Jewish Intercommunal Organization,' *PAAJR (Proceedings of the American Academy for Jewish Research)* 36 (1968), pp. 13–31.

Chazan, R., *Medieval Jewry in Northern France*, Baltimore 1973.

Chazan, R., 'From Friar Paul to Friar Raymond: The Development of Innovative Missionizing Argumentation,' *Harvard Theological Review* 73 (1983), pp. 289–306.

Chazan, R., *European Jewry and the First Crusade*, Berkeley 1987.

Chazan, R., 'The Condemnation of the Talmud Reconsidered (1239–1248),' *PAAJR (Proceedings of the American Academy for Jewish Research)* 55 (1988), pp. 11–30.

Chazan, R., 'Factivity of Medieval Narrative: A Case Study of the Hebrew First Crusade Narrative,' *Association for Jewish Studies Review* 16 (1991), pp. 31–56.

Chazan, R., *God, Humanity, and History: The Hebrew First Crusade Narratives*, Berkeley 2000.

Chazan, R., *The Jews of Medieval Western Christendom 1000–1500*, Cambridge 2006.

Cohen, J., *The Friars and the Jews*, Ithaca 1982.

Cohen, J., 'The Mentality of the Medieval Jewish Apostate: Peter Alfonsi, Hermann of Cologne and Pablo Christiani,' in: *Jewish Apostasy in the Modern World*, ed. T. M. Endelman, New York 1987, pp. 20–47.

Cohen, J., 'Between Martyrdom and Apostasy: Doubt and Self-Definition in the Twelfth-Century Ashkenaz,' *Journal of Medieval and Early Modern Studies* 29 (1999), pp. 431–471.

Cohen, J., 'The Second Disputation of Paris and its Place in Thirteenth Century Jewish Christian Polemic,' [Hebrew] *Tarbiz* 68 (1999), pp. 557–579.

Cohen, J., *Sanctifying the Name of God*, Philadelphia 2004.

Colorni, V., *Legge ebraica e leggi locali*, Milan 1945.

Cramer, P., *Baptism and Change in the Early Middle Ages, 200–1150,* Cambridge 1993.

David, A., 'Programs against French Jewry during the Shepherd's Crusade of 1251,' [Hebrew] *Tarbiz* 46 (1977), pp. 251–257.

Davidson, I., *Thesaurus of Medieval Jewish Poetry* [Hebrew], 4 vols. New York 1970.

Eliade, M., *Rites and Symbols of Initiation: The Mysteries of Birth and Rebirth*, New York 1965.

Elukin, J., 'From Jew to Christian? Conversion and Immutability in Medieval Europe,' in: *Varieties of Religious Conversion in the Middle Ages*, ed. J. Muldoon, Gainesville, Fla. 1997, pp. 171–189.

Elukin, J., 'The Discovery of the Self: Jews and Conversion in the Twelfth Century,' in: *Jews and Christians in Twelfth-Century Europe*, eds. Michael Signer and John Van Engen, Notre Dame, Ind. 2001, pp. 63–76.

Elukin, J., *Living Together Living Apart*, Princeton 2007.

Emanuel, S., *Fragments of the Tablets: Lost Books of the Tosaphists* [Hebrew], Jerusalem 2006.

Fram, E., 'Perception and Reception of Repentant Apostates in Medieval Ashkenaz and Premodern Poland,' *Association for Jewish Studies Review* 21 (1996), pp. 299–339.

Furst, R., 'Captivity, Conversion, and Communal Identity: Sexual Angst and Religious Crisis in Frankfurt, 1241,' *Jewish History* 2 (2008), pp. 179–221.

Golb, N., 'Notes on the Conversion of European Christians to Judaism in the Eleventh Century,' *Journal of Jewish Studies* 16 (1965), pp. 69–74.

Goldin, S., 'The Socialisation for "Kidush ha-Shem" among Medieval Jews,' *Journal of Medieval History* 23 (1997), pp. 117–138.

Goldin, S., 'Juifs et juifs convertis au Moyen Age: "Es-tu encore mon frére?,"' *Annales, Histoire, Sciences Sociales* 54 (1999), pp. 851–874.

Goldin, S., 'Jewish Society under Pressure: The Concept of Childhood,' in: *Youth in the Middle Ages*, eds. P. J. Goldberg and F. Riddy, York 2004, pp. 25–43.

Goldin, S., *The Ways of Jewish Martyrdom*, Turnhout 2008.

Goldin, S., *Jewish Women in Europe in the Middle Ages: A Quiet Revolution*, Manchester 2011.

Grayzel, S., *The Church and the Jews in the XIIIth Century*, rev. edition, New York 1966.

Grayzel, S., 'Popes, Jews, and Inquisition: From "Sicut" to "Torbato corde,"' *Essays on the Occasion of the Seventieth Anniversary of the Dropsie University (1909–1979)*, eds. A. Katsh and L. Nemoy, Philadelphia 1977, pp. 151–188.

Grossman, A., *The Early Sages of Ashkenaz* [Hebrew], Jerusalem 1981.

Grossman, A., *The Early Sages of France* [Hebrew], Jerusalem 1995.

Grossman, A., 'Saladin's Victory and the Aliya of the Jews of Europe to the Land of Israel,' [Hebrew] in: *Studies in the History of Eretz Israel, Presented to Yehuda Ben Porat*, eds. Y. Ben-Arieh and E. Reiner, Jerusalem 2003, pp. 361–381.

Grossman, A., 'A Typological Legend about the Conversion of the Son of R. Gershom Me'or ha-Gola,' [Hebrew] in: *Studies in Jewish Narrative, Ma`aseh Sippur, Presented to Yoav Elstein*, eds. A. Lipsker and R. Kushelevsky, Ramat Gan 2006, pp. 65–75.

Haverkamp, A., 'Baptised Jews in German Lands during the Twelfth Century,' in: *Jews and Christians in Twelfth Century Europe*, eds. M. A. Signer and J. Van Engen, Notre Dame, Ind. 2001, pp. 255–310.

Haverkamp, E., *Hebraische Berichte uber die Judenverfolgungen wahrend des ersten Kreuzzugs, Monumenta Germaniae historica. Hebraische Texte aus dem mittelalterlichenDeutschland*, Hannover 2005.

Heil, J., 'Agobard, Amolo, das Kirchengut und die Juden von Lyon,' *Francia* 25 (1998), pp. 39–76.

Horowitz, E., 'Medieval Jews Face the Cross,' in: *Facing the Cross*, eds. Y. T. Assis, J. Cohen, A. Kedar et al., Jerusalem 2000, pp. 118–140.

Irshai, O., 'The Apostate as an Inheritor in Geonic Responsa: Basics of Decision Making and Parallels in Gentile Law,' *Shenaton ha-Mishpat ha-Ivri* 11–12 (1984–86), pp. 435–462.

Jordan, W. C., *The French Monarchy and the Jews: From Philip Augustus to the Last Capetians*, Philadelphia 1989.

Jordan, W. C., 'Adolescence and Conversion in the Middle Ages: A Research Agenda,' in: *Jews and Christians in Twelfth-Century Europe*, eds. M. A. Signer and J. Van Engen, Notre Dame, Ind. 2001, pp. 77–93.

Kanarfogel, E., 'Returning to the Jewish Community in Medieval Ashkenaz: History and Halakhah,' in: *Turim*, Studies in Jewish History and Literature Presented to Dr. Bernard Lander, Vol. 1, ed. M. A. Shmidman, New York 2007, pp. 69–97.

Katz, J., 'Even Though a Sinner, He is Still of Israel,' [Hebrew] *Tarbiz* 27 (1958), pp. 203–227.

Katz, J., *Exclusiveness and Tolerance*, Oxford 1961.

Kleinberg, A., 'Hermanus Judaeos Opusculum: In Defence of its Authenticity,' *Revue des études juives* 151 (1992), pp. 337–353.

Kupfer, E., 'A Contribution to the Chronicles of the Family of R. Moses Ben Yom-Tov "the Noble" of London,' [Hebrew] *Tarbiz* 40 (1971), pp. 385–387.

Langmuir, G., *Towards a Definition of Antisemitism*, Los Angeles 1990.

Lavee, M., 'Converting the Missionary Image of Abraham: Rabbinic Traditions Migrating from the Land of Israel to Babylon,' in: *Abraham, the Nations, and the Hagarites: Jewish, Christian, and Islamic Perspectives on Kinship with Abraham*, eds. M. Goodman, G. van Kooten, and J. van Ruiten, Lieden 2011, pp. 203–222.

Lavie, M., '"A Convert is Like a Newborn Child": The Concept and its Implications in Rabbinic Literature,' [Hebrew] PhD Thesis, Ben-Gurion University of the Negev 2003.

Linder A., 'Christlich-Jüdische Konfrontation im kirchlichen Frühmittelalter,' in: *Kirchengeschichte als Missionsgeschichte* Vol. 2 *Die Kirche des frühen Mittelalters*, Munich 1978, pp. 397–441.

Linder, A., *Roman Imperial Legislation on the Jews* [Hebrew], Jerusalem 1983.

Loeb, I., 'La controverse de 1240 sur le Talmud,' *Revue des études juives* 1 (1880), pp. 247–261, 2 (1881), pp. 248–270, 3 (1883), pp. 39–57.

Malkiel, D., 'Destruction or Conversion: Intention and Reaction: Crusaders and Jews, in 1096,' *Jewish History* 15 (2001), pp. 257–280.

Marcus, I. G., 'Review of Robert Chazan, "European Jewry and the First Crusade,"' *Speculum* 64 (1989), pp. 685–688.

Marcus, I. G., 'History, Story and Collective Memory: Narrativity in Early Ashkenazic Culture,' *Prooftexts* 10 (1990), pp. 365–388.

Merchavia, C., *The Church Versus Talmudic and Midrashic Literature 500–1248* [Hebrew], Jerusalem 1970 pp, 227–360.

Merchavia, C., 'Did Nicholas Donin Instigate the Blood Libel?' [Hebrew] *Tarbiz* 49 (1980), pp. 11–121.

Müller-Mertens, E., 'The Ottonians as Kings and Emperors,' in: *The New Cambridge Medieval History*, Vol. 3, ed. T. Reuter, Cambridge 1999, pp. 233–266.

Mundill, R., *England's Jewish Solution*, Cambridge 1998.

Noble, S., 'The Jewish Woman in Medieval Martyrology,' *Studies in Jewish Bibliography, History and Literature in Honor of I. E. Kiev*, ed. C. Berlin, New York 1971, pp. 347–355. (Also in: *Proceedings of the Fifth World Congress of the Jewish Studies* 2 (1972), pp. 133–140).

Pakter, W. J., *Medieval Canon Law and the Jews*, Ebelsbach am Main 1988.

Panitz, J. M., 'Conversion to Judaism in the Middle Ages: Historic Patterns and New Scenarios,' *Conservative Judaism* 36 (1983), p. 46.

Parkes, J. W., *The Conflict of the Church and the Synagogue*, London 1934.

Pegues, F. J., *The Lawyers of the Last Capetians*, Princeton 1962.

Perry, M., *Tradition and Transformation: Knowledge Transmission among European Jews in the Middle Ages*, Tel Aviv 2010.

Pohl, W., 'Telling the Difference: Signs of Ethnic Identity,' in: *Strategies of Distinction: The Contracting of Ethnic Communities, 300–900*, ed. W Pohl with H. Reimitz, Leiden 1998, pp. 17–69.

Porton, G., *The Stranger Within Your Gates*, Chicago 1994.

Prinz, J., *Popes from the Ghetto*, New York 1968.

Raspe, L., 'Payyetanim as Heroes of Medieval Folk Narrative: The Case of R. Shimon B. Yishaq of Mainz,' in: The Schaefer Festschrift: *Jewish Studies Between the Disciplines / Judaistik zwischen den Disziplinen: Papers in Honor of Peter Schäfer on the Occasion of his Sixtieth Birthday*, eds. K. Herrmann, M. Schlüter, and G. Veltri, Leiden 2003, pp. 354–369.

Raspe, L., *Jüdische Hagiographie im mittelalterlichen Aschkenas*, Tübingen 2006.

Reiner, A., 'L'attitude envers les proselytes en Allemagne et en France du XIe au XIIIe Siecle,' *Revue des études juives* 167 (2008), pp. 99–119.

Rosenthal, J. M., 'The Talmud on Trial: The Disputation at Paris in the Year 1240,' *Jewish Quarterly Review* 47 (1956–57), pp. 58–76 and 145–169.

Rubin, M., *Gentile Tales: The Narrative Assault on Late Medieval Jews*, London 1999.

Saltman, A., 'Hermann's *Opusculum de conversion sua*: Truth or Fiction?' *Revue des études juives* 147 (1988), pp. 31–56.

Schmitt J. C., 'La memoire de Premontre: a propos de l'autobiographie du Premontre Herman le Juif,' in: *La vie des moines et chanoines reguliers au Moyen Age et temps modernes*, ed. M. Derwich, Wroclaw 1995, pp. 439–452.

Shatzmiller, J., 'Did Nicholas Donin Promulgate the Blood Libel?' [Hebrew] *Mehkarim* 4 (1978), pp. 173–182.

Shatzmiller, J., *La deuxième controverse de Paris: un capitre dans la polemique entre Chretiens et Juifs au Moyen Age* (Collection de la REJ, 15), Paris 1994.

Simonsohn, S., *The Apostolic See and the Jews*, Toronto 1991.

Soloveitchik, H., 'Three Thems in Sefer Hasidim,' *Association for Jewish Studies Review* 1 (1976), pp. 311–357.

Stacey, R. C., 'The Conversion of Jews to Christianity in Thirteenth-Century England,' *Speculum* 67 (1992), pp. 263–283.

Stow, K., 'Conversion, Apostasy, and Apprehensiveness: Emicho of Flonheim and the Fear of Jews in the Twelfth Century,' *Speculum* 76 (2001), pp. 911–933.

Toch, M., *Die Juden im mittelalterlichen Reich*, Munich 1998.

Urbach, E. E., *The Tosaphists: Their History, Writings and Methods*, Jerusalem 1980.

Van Gennep, A., *The Rites of Passage*, London 1960.

Voltmer, E., 'Die Juden in den mittelalterlichen Städten des Rheingebiets,' in: *Juden in der Stadt*, eds. F. Mayrhofer and F. Opll, Linz 1999, pp. 119–143.

Yuval, I. J., *Two Nations in Your Womb*, Berkeley 2006.

Index